Pathways Through Writing Blocks in the Academic Environment

Pathways Through Writing Blocks in the Academic Environment

Kate Evans MA
www.writingourselveswell.co.uk

SENSE PUBLISHERS
ROTTERDAM/BOSTON/TAIPEI

A C.I.P. record for this book is available from the Library of Congress.

ISBN: 978-94-6209-241-9 (paperback)
ISBN: 978-94-6209-142-9 (hardback)
ISBN: 978-94-6209-242-6 (e-book)

Published by: Sense Publishers,
P.O. Box 21858,
3001 AW Rotterdam,
The Netherlands
https://www.sensepublishers.com/

Printed on acid-free paper

All Rights Reserved © 2013 Sense Publishers

No part of this work may be reproduced, stored in a retrieval system, or transmitted in any form or by any means, electronic, mechanical, photocopying, microfilming, recording or otherwise, without written permission from the Publisher, with the exception of any material supplied specifically for the purpose of being entered and executed on a computer system, for exclusive use by the purchaser of the work.

TABLE OF CONTENTS

Foreword: Dr Linda Finlay — vii

Acknowledgements — xi

Introduction
Orienteering: Finding a Starting Point for Our Pathway Through Our Writing Block — 1

1. Entering the Labyrinth: The "Creative Process" and the "Creative Attitude" in Academic Writing — 9

2. Hazardous Ground: The Relational and Emotional Aspects of Writing Blocks within the Academic Environment — 37

3. A Viewpoint: The Craft of Gaining Perspective in Academic Writing — 55

4. Finding the Story: The InterPlay Between Narrative and Writing Blocks — 69

5. Academic Writing: New Approaches: Conventions and New Approaches in Academic Writing — How They Impact Writing Blocks — 83

6. Creative Academic Writing: How "Creative" Techniques Can Facilitate Academic Writing — 101

7. Case Studies: Experiences of Writing Blocks Within the Academic Environment — 115

Conclusion: A Place to Rest — 137

Appendix: The Gestalt Cycle — 139

References — 141

Index — 147

DR LINDA FINLAY

FOREWORD

As I sit down to write this, I'm aware of my own hesitation, my reluctance, to begin the process of setting down words. Part of me is enjoying the irony of encountering writer's block while preparing a foreword to a book dealing with that very problem. Then I remember Kate Evans's counsel that writing, as a creative process with an emotional component, always requires time. I urge myself to pause, to reflect…

> I see myself walking down a corridor. There is a door to my right; I open it and I enter a room full of people. Their voices sing out in chorus: "You're only an academic — you can't write! Who do you think you are, writing an introduction to a book on writing? Don't let Kate down; this is too important to mess up! You're not going to be able to do justice to her work." …Feeling sick in my stomach, I look for a way out. There is a door opposite. I crack it open cautiously. To my relief, I'm greeted with a friendly, reassuring chorus: "You know you can write, Linda — you've written loads of books and articles! Kate invited you, so she believes in you. What an honour! Do it for her! You know what you want — and need — to say, so just say it!"
>
> Then I hear Kate's voice: "Give yourself time to amass material without pressure to produce." Yes, thank you, Kate. I feel my tension, my "block", dissipate. I welcome my "Waiting-Muse" (Kate's phrase) and offer her more nourishment. With the pressure now off, I allow myself space to dwell with the book and jot down notes as they occur to me. I remind myself that my foreword doesn't need to be "perfect". Nor does the writing have to be outstanding. I soon realise my corridor has opened out to become a vista, a landscape criss-crossed with paths I can explore. I begin to relish the challenge before me. I feel ready to begin, ready to think about writing.…

Kate Evans's book: *Pathways Through Writing Blocks in the Academic Environment*, ranges far beyond the development of academic writing skills to explore the barriers that can block the path of anyone attempting to write. To this end, the author takes us on a journey, supplying us with appropriate maps and a compass to help us navigate our way. We learn, perhaps to our surprise, that even academic writing demands and involves the creative process. We are shown ways to engage academic writing at a practical level and to identify those strategies that work for us individually. Along the way we are invited to dialogue with parts of our self and examine our own emotional process: for example, the potential shame, tensions and resistances which may provoke our writing blocks. Most importantly, Kate offers us sure-footed routes out of those all too familiar "swamps": the moments when, overwhelmed by data or unsure of where we are headed, we slip, get stuck, and sink.

The book's clear structure gives readers the freedom to dip into particular issues or read from beginning to end. Its chapters address specific topics: for instance, how to understand the emotional component of academic writing, and how to see the writing project in terms of a "story". The chapters are tied together by sections examining the nature of writing block and offering practical strategies to overcome it.

There are many gems to be savoured as Kate weaves her tales, incorporating her own personal reflections. My favourite chapter is the "Case Studies" one where we hear of Kate's research on the lived experience of several individuals who have, in different ways, struggled to write academically. Using powerful images and metaphors, the author beautifully captures each battle. She also offers a wise analysis of the nature of that person's particular writing block. These stories struck a chord with my own stumbling progress towards becoming an academic writer.

One important message from this book is that our writing blocks may well have something useful to tell us, be it about our writing or about ourselves as academic "writers". As Kate emphasises, writing is a skill that can be developed by paying attention to the creative writing process and to nurturing a self-aware (reflexive) relationship with our own writing.

It is reassuring to know that all writers are vulnerable to blocks. Where do these "dragons" (Kate's phrase) come from? Are critical voices from our past lurking in our memories? Are we struggling to come to terms with a new identity as an academic writer? Is it even right to assume that these writing "dragons" are our enemy? Perhaps, Kate suggests, they are simply trying to protect us. It's worth getting to know those parts of ourselves which try to keep us safe from exposure. Then we can become more positive about, and active in, our relationship with our writing.

Often, the author argues, the way forward involves moving fluidly between the extremes of being too close to the writing and being too distant and uninvolved. It's important to nurture a writing habit (a daily reflective diary can be a useful exercise) and to be patient of the mess as we allow our writing to evolve iteratively. To help us, Kate offers numerous suggestions; for instance, using imagery, brainstorm lists or pattern notes to spark inspiration. She takes us through a variety of creative writing exercises she has found useful when helping students improve their writing and find their voice. The value of creating a "fairy tale" to find the narrative within a particular piece of writing was something I had never considered before.

This book offers something for every academic writer, whether budding or experienced. Students struggling with essays and dissertations will find many practical exercises along with invaluable advice. More practised writers will encounter fresh insights; for example, into why we avoid certain types of writing and how we might overcome that tendency. Self-awareness and growth, suggest the author, are intertwined with the development of our own writing "voice".

FOREWORD

I am confident that you, the reader, will enjoy this book, which is itself a model of good writing. Its clear, flowing style will draw you in, and you will relish Kate's use of poetic metaphors and her readiness for self-disclosure; her writing is both engaging and unpretentious. The many practical exercises are excellent, worthwhile and enjoyable, while the summary boxes included at regular intervals effectively reinforce key messages.

Kate's varied professional background — as a writer, an academic, a creative writing teacher and a psychotherapeutic counsellor — gives her a unique vantage point. Her wide-ranging scholarly references open up the field in novel and intriguing ways but at the same time she remains present as a human being. Time and again when reading the book I was struck by her sensitive permission-giving and empathy; she becomes our enabler, subtly encouraging and guiding our literary self-development. As I read, I feel in safe, knowledgeable hands: hands which hold my more vulnerable "emotional self" while stimulating my "writer self" and giving me permission to write in my own way. Her exercises, revelatory and often fun, take me beyond the dry, standard rules of academic writing. I feel spoken to in a direct, appreciative and knowing way.

…I return to my "corridor" and feel brave enough to open both doors. I allow my "encouraging chorus" to meet and greet my "critical chorus"; somehow the latter voices are quiet now. I thank all of them for helping to support me. I tell them that I've enjoyed writing this piece and that I've made intriguing discoveries along the way. I celebrate the renewal of my writing. And for this I thank Kate.

ACKNOWLEDGEMENTS

Thank you to everyone who has made this book possible, to everyone who took the time to ask, "How's it going?" and to keep me supplied with tea and cakes. In particular, my deepest gratitude goes to those who gave freely of their time and their understanding. To those who contributed to this book, through interview, via email, by sending over that article, through discussion. To my lovely and patient readers: Ros Evans, Dr Linda Finlay, Dr Lesley Glover, Felix Hodcroft, Lydia Noor and Louise Richardson. I owe you much. Thank you to Dr Linda Finlay for her foreword. Thanks to Rufus, Dan and Annie for allowing me to unravel and heal. I am indebted to the writers who continue to inspire me. I am grateful to Peter de Liefde for taking a punt. And thank you to my husband, Mark, whose love and belief in me as a writer has sustained me over the years.

Proofreading by Jenny Drewery: jdrewery.thewriterthebetter@gmail.com

INTRODUCTION

ORIENTEERING

Finding a Starting Point for Our Pathway Through Our Writing Block

This book is aimed at people who want to write within the academic environment. Perhaps you are an undergraduate struggling with essays, or a PhD student feeling stuck with a chapter of your thesis, or an academic who knows there's an article you need to write, but you're forever putting it off? Maybe you are an academic who has already been published and yet still finds it hard to get on with the book you know is within you somewhere? Or you are a supervisor or colleague of someone who is stymied in their academic writing and your usual supportive strategies are proving fruitless? My intention is that there will be something in this book for all of you. It could be a small suggestion or insight which sets the ball rolling, or it could be the larger invitation running through the book to engage with developing as an academic writer.

For those tackling academic writing, there is advice in abundance, whether it comes from tutors, peers, study advice, or "how-to" guidance in articles or books. These are all valuable resources to turn to again and again. This book does not seek to replace. Instead this book wishes to complement what is already available, by taking a particular approach, namely:

- Our writing blocks have something useful to tell us, either about our writing or about ourselves as writers.
- Writing is a skill that can be developed.
- Writing, even writing academically, is a creative act.
- The majority of writing blocks are multifaceted and have an emotional element to them.

WRITING BLOCKS CAN BE USEFUL

I am at this moment hesitant to go on. I know this to be true and yet I wonder if I could ever persuade a reader who has an assignment to complete by the next day of its veracity. Being stuck, being blocked, is not a pleasant feeling; and then to be told, "Well, this is actually useful," could potentially be very annoying indeed. So I am risking my readers' wrath by insisting, our writing blocks may have something constructive to tell us.

Our writing blocks could be "signposts" (Palumbo, 2000, p. 17) to new information about ourselves as writers (see Chapters 2 & 5 and Case Studies 1 & 2) and about our material (see Chapter 3 & Case Study 2).

INTRODUCTION

What is interesting to note at this point is the power of belief (often borne of previous experience) in the human psyche (DeYoung, 2003; Clarkson, 2003). Allowing the possibility that our writing block may be a useful tool for insight could already lessen its capacity to hinder us.

WRITING IS A SKILL THAT CAN BE DEVELOPED

No-one is born a writer. Writing is a skill that can be learnt. Often in the academic arena, too little attention is given to how people acquire the skill of writing, as if students, researchers, academics will enter the field fully fledged in their penmanship (Antoniou & Moriarty, 2008; Newnes & Jones, 2005). This is not so. Academic writers require nurturing. They require an "apprenticeship". An "apprentice" writer has models to work from, they have support, they have the opportunity to practise and make mistakes, they are allowed to work up from, say, writing a letter to a journal or a review before trying something more complex and challenging. Without this apprenticeship, some will flounder, finding their writing blocked.

I enjoy yoga, I take a class once a week, I have done so over a number of years. I am certainly better at yoga now than I was when I first came to the group; on the other hand, I know I could improve more if I practised and attended further classes. I choose not to. I have chosen the skill level I am going to stick at; it suits me. So it is with writing. We can select the skill level which works for us. The more time, practice, effort and commitment we are able and prepared to give to honing our writing skills, the more fluent, flexible and available our writing style will become, allowing us to express what we want, when we want, in a voice that has resonance and authenticity. However, even with a modicum of perseverance with our writing apprenticeship we can find that the words flow more easily for us. See Chapters 1 & 5 for more.

> It is the experience and hard work of every day which alone will ripen in the long run and allow one to do something truer and more complete. ... You will not always do well, but the days you least expect it, you will do that which holds its own with the work of those that have gone before. (Vincent Van Gogh in Olsen, 1978, p. 13.)

WRITING IS A CREATIVE ACT

All writing — academic or otherwise — is a creative act. This means two things. Firstly, getting to know our own creative process will aid us to write academically with greater facility (see Chapter 1). It may be that what we are naming a block — a moment when we are unable to put words onto the paper or computer screen — is not a block at all. It is part of our creative rhythm. If we sit and force ourselves to be in front of the blank page or screen we are fighting against our natural way of doing things; this may reinforce our sense that we are blocked, making it even more difficult to face our work the next time. Secondly, it means we can engage creative writing techniques to assist us to write more easily and effectively (see exercises throughout the book, plus Chapters 4, 5 & 6).

I am a proponent of the "Slow Language Movement" (Laird, 2009) where language matters and it is "neither disposable nor simply denotative", it takes time to compose (how funny: I initially typed "compost" here) as well as to read and digest. Creative writing techniques take us gently into the Slow Language Movement. Though we may not be writing rapidly, we are writing sustainably, we are writing to discover what we do not already know and giving ourselves permission to dwell and play awhile to uncover new meanings. In using metaphor we are keying into a human process to find meaning and give richness to an experience. In writing creatively, we are honouring the depth and complexity of our material and of the world we are a part of.

I am very much aware, however, that many of my readers will be interested in something more "quick fix". And throughout the book I have tips on creative writing techniques which are more fast-acting. It is also the case that, as with anything, the more proficiency we develop with a skill, the quicker we are able to put it into play. So some time spent now increasing our familiarity and aptitude with creative writing techniques could save time in the future as we avoid blocks and write with greater competence.

WRITING BLOCKS HAVE AN EMOTIONAL ELEMENT

Working in the academic environment, we are supposed to be rational, logical beings, functioning cognitively. We put our emotions aside. Right? Wrong. Or at least, certainly not when we are talking about writing blocks. Chapter 2 explores the emotional underpinnings of many writing blocks. It will be for many a difficult chapter to read; however, I do think it is one worth persevering with. I also believe it is important to ask for support while doing so. The case studies in Chapter 7 also show how alive and multifaceted the psychological elements of writing blocks can be. My purpose in bringing these aspects into the light is to offer insight. It is with insight and support that we can begin to address how our feelings affect our capacity to keep writing.

HOW TO READ THIS BOOK

Everyone who writes has moments when they feel blocked. This may be to do with their creative process (Chapter 1), to do with their emotional state (Chapter 2) or to do with the need to develop their skills (Chapters 1 and 3-6). As academics who write, we are no different. Though some generalisations can be made — and I do make them — each person's writing block is individual and the approach they need to find will, therefore, be specific to them.

INTRODUCTION

Throughout this book I have used the metaphor of a map. We are moving through a writerly landscape and each of us will find our own pathway, the way which is most useful to us personally. I have used the metaphor of the map and the short snippets of storytelling at the beginning of each chapter in order to give permission to roam as we please, while also offering some gentle orientation. I have also employed the metaphor of the map and the storytelling because they are creative techniques and I want to illustrate the power of creative techniques within the academic paradigm.

So read this book as you will. Read the whole thing from cover to cover or choose a chapter which seems to hook you in or dip in and dip out. Draw on this book in a way which is most useful for you. These are suggestions of approaches and exercises which have worked for me and I have seen work for others. However, I have often adapted them from how they were first offered to me, so I expect you to do the same, adjust them to your own particular sense of what will help you develop and flourish. You will read this book in ways that I cannot imagine. And how wonderful is that. That is, indeed, the wonder of writing, that others can connect with your words and take them in unenvisioned directions.

READ THIS FIRST!

I expect you will find your own way around this book. However, I would suggest that you read this section and the "The Academic Writing Apprenticeship" section under "Writing Strategies" in Chapter 1 before going on.

I do believe that the writing approaches and exercises proposed here are potentially useful in working with writing blocks. Nevertheless, I do feel the need to give a word of warning. Writing, especially using some of the more "unconscious" methods put forward in this book, can be very powerful. It can excavate below defences that we have quite rightly put in place to shield us from psychological pain (DeYoung, 2003). It can do so without us really being aware that is the direction we are going in, especially at the beginning. I advise going gently, turning the page where necessary and seeking support when needed.

Here I want to highlight two further aspects essential for the reading of this book:

– Guidelines for tackling the writing exercises.
– Reflexivity.

Guidelines for Tackling the Writing Exercises

– Do them as quickly as you can.
– Spend maybe 30 minutes on exercises, certainly no more than an hour, before moving on to your other tasks of the day.
– Something which is imperfect and not quite finished is the expected outcome.
– If you find yourself not wanting to do one of the exercises, note what you are thinking and feeling and what is going on in your body, write as much of this as

you can then move on, either to a different exercise or on to your other tasks of the day.
– Something — a word, a phrase or an insight — may come out of these exercises immediately. On the other hand, this may not happen. Both outcomes are good.
– Whatever happens, what you write is material for you to give consideration to at a later date (see below "Reflexivity").
– In general, I am suggesting that you keep what you write in your writing journal (see "The Academic Writing Apprenticeship" section under "Writing Strategies" in Chapter 1). Though you may decide that you want to get rid of certain pieces or destroy them, perhaps as a symbolic destruction of the writing block you have identified, I would advise against being too quick to throw away your writing. This in itself may be suggestive of undervaluing your work. I would propose that any writing you do inspired by the exercises in this book is ripe for the reflexive endeavour discussed below.
– Enjoy, have fun, be sad, be happy, be angry, have a laugh. Be curious without being judgemental. We can be seriously working without getting too serious.
– Share as much of this experience as you can with supportive others even if you choose not to share what you are actually writing.

Reflexivity

> A discovery of some of the creative writing tools ... [has] begun to inform the way I think about writing and support my own writing processes. The added bonus for me as I engaged with creative writing was to experience its power as a reflective tool. (Helen Atkin, personal communication.)

A "reflective tool"? This is something which encourages a contemplation of a subject, a taking the time to turn it over and see it from many angles, a breathing space within action which allows for evaluation and learning. I have chosen the word "reflexivity" which, as defined by Finlay (2011), brings the researcher into the process. It invites us to be self-aware and thoughtful about our own role in constructing not only the analysis but also the data. Reflexivity allows for the postmodern context: the acknowledgement of the researcher's place in the research; the subjective (rather than objective) stance; and relative and constructed knowledge (all of which are explored further in this book).

Reflexivity is iterative: we revisit material over again, unpick it, looking for underlying implicit meanings. Each visit increases our understanding and adds another layer or perspective to our material. Reflexivity is gently noticing and evaluative rather than harshly judgemental. We are interested in what is happening, curious about it, watching, rather than quick to assessment and decision. Reflexivity allows for possibilities, even ones which don't immediately seem to warrant consideration.

INTRODUCTION

I would encourage this open, reflexive attitude for reading this book in general, but in particular when any of the writing exercises are attempted. These writing exercises are designed to give us new information either about why we are finding it hard to write or about the material we are working with. Sometimes the one feeds into the other: something in the material is making it hard for us to write, or by identifying what is blocking us we understand our work to a greater extent.

Writing in itself can be a reflexive act. We can pay attention to the words written down. What words are puzzling to us? What words have impact on us? What words are repeated? Being aware of the "creative" writing techniques described throughout the book — such as word sounds and identifying metaphor — can assist us in unearthing deeper understandings. These techniques offer one lens for analysing our material and also our sense of ourselves as writers. By being more familiar with them, we can use them more effectively to offer greater clarity.

The main aspect of reflexive writing to bear in mind is that it is about noticing rather than judging. We are not assessing the quality of our writing, or even whether its content could be termed "right" or "wrong". We are noticing what we have written and we are enquiring about what meanings we might find there and our attendant feelings. We may be able to have this attitude as soon as we have written something; on the other hand, we might need to wait and come back to it, to see it with fresher eyes. We are not acting as a critic; on the other hand, if we feel critical, it is worth noting and wondering whether this sense of criticism is rooted in a particular attitude towards our writing or our topic. Has criticism always come to the surface when we write? Is it our own or does it come from someone else in our life? Or is criticism somehow connected to the subject of our writing? We can be reflexive about critical thoughts and feelings without allowing them to stop us in our tracks.

Thompson (in Bolton, Howlett, Lago & Wright, 2004, p. 82) suggests a feedback loop, which starts with questions such as:

When I read this:
– I notice…
– I am surprised that…
– I realise…

As I read this:
– I am aware that…
– I feel…

What emerges from this kind of questioning can be written about or discussed with trusted colleagues until there is "recognition" and "owning" of the meanings which are arising. The creative writing exercises can be used once again to explore the reflexive musings, and then the "feedback loop" questions are posed and so on until new understandings emerge. Once this begins to happen, some "integrating" can occur, allowing for the acceptance of the options we have taken and/or for the possibility of different perspectives and choices as we go along.

For example, when I first began to write about the anxieties I have around writing, they became a rather nasty, toad-like creature, waiting under slimy rocks ready to pounce and bring me down. However, using the reflexive feedback loop, I began to realise that far from being malicious, my toad was trying to keep me safe, stop me from "making a fool of myself". This realisation already lessened the anxiety; it also helped the writing process to be less fraught and conflictual. I still sometimes have to reassure my toad — that anxious part of myself — (often through getting encouragement from trusted friends) that an audience could be pretty unkind but it is unlikely to actually tear me limb from limb.

TAKING THE FIRST STEP

The map is laid out. We have our walking boots on. During our journey there may be some false starts and dead ends, as well as some laughs and stunning vistas. We have put some thought into who might be prepared to be our fellow travellers. We have our reflexivity compass to hand. We might be ready for a quick foray to pick up some tips, or we may be preparing for the long haul. We are novices or seasoned trekkers. Whatever our starting point or our final destination, we are ready to step out and find our own pathways through our writing blocks.

CHAPTER 1

ENTERING THE LABYRINTH

The "Creative Process" and the "Creative Attitude" in Academic Writing

We have entered a labyrinth. It is our own labyrinth, so we can plan it out how we wish. It can be changed as we go along. The walls are dark-green yew or perhaps smooth white plaster; it is for us to define. They twist and turn. There are places for us to rest and there are refreshing resources — good food to eat, books to read, exquisite works of art, a profundity of sweet-smelling vegetation, music sifting through the warm air. At other points there is less illumination, more uncertainty about the direction of the corridors. We hesitate, we ponder, our movement forward is arrested. Yet, as with all labyrinths, its ways inexorably take us to the centre where there is a lit hearth and nourishment, a place to work, a place to sleep, the carefully wrapped gifts of insight and inspiration left especially for us. Each time we enter our labyrinth we may remake it, though as we become more familiar with the journey the path will become more fixed, even if it remains flexible. And if we look thoroughly as we travel through our labyrinth, there is the guiding golden thread which will show us the way in and help us find our way out again.

INTRODUCTION

When we write within the academic environment we in effect enter into a "creative process"; we inevitably engage with our creativity. If we are unaware of how our creativity functions or what our creativity might need in order to survive and flourish, then we may find our writing hand coming to a halt. In this chapter, firstly I justify my statement that an academic writing task entails a "creative process". Secondly I describe one way of conceptualising the "creative process"; in other words, what happens for us when we take on that academic writing task. Thirdly I will look at what constitutes a "creative approach". Then, having clarified what I mean by the "creative process" and the "creative approach", I look at how blocks to writing might occur within this context. We may discover that some blocks are not blocks at all, but rather an essential component to the way we write. They only become blocks because they are not recognised for what they really are. Finally in this chapter, I will explore some strategies for overcoming writing blocks associated with the "creative process" and the "creative approach".

CHAPTER 1

I'm imagining some of my readers already baulking at the thought of spending time reading this chapter. "A creative process?" I hear you cry. "How can wasting a moment on that help me finish my essay due in three days' time?" "A creative process?" I hear you object. "My field isn't writing; this feels like a huge subject and sidetrack from what I ought to be studying." Ah, but, I counter, reading this chapter and then spending just ten minutes considering it could save you hours of fruitless effort in the future. Becoming even a little bit more conversant with the mechanics of our own individual creative process could already help push a block to one side. For instance, just noticing we write better at a particular time of day may be revelation enough to get us through the next deadline. Then we can continually pay attention to our creative process in small ways, stoking and fostering it. This will be of assistance for the long haul. When an amateur runner decides to take on the challenge of a marathon, they put aside small allotments of time to train and develop their fitness. So, if we develop our capacity as a writer even in minor ways, for instance by using the exercises at the end of this chapter for fifteen minutes every other day, then, subsequently, when essays loom or chapters have to be presented to supervisors, the writing will flow more easily.

In this chapter, I will consider:

– How academic writing is an inherently creative process.
– How the creative process can be characterised.
– How writing can bind the creative process together, be our "golden thread" into and out of the labyrinth.
– What is meant by a "creative approach".

I will suggest that having a clearer understanding of our own individual creative process and of a creative approach can explain halts in our writing. And finally, I will propose strategies for working with our creative process and our creative approach and, thereby, with any blocks which might be associated with it.

ACADEMIC WRITING, A "CREATIVE PROCESS"?

Firstly, however, to the question: How can I say that academic writing is part of a "creative process"? What do I mean by the words "creative" and "process"? Neither are easily pinned down. When connected with writing, the word creative is most often linked with the imagination, fiction, artistry or flights of fancy. None of which sits comfortably with academia. Here, though, I will be concentrating on other aspects of the word creative, for example, to be resourceful, inventive and productive. There is room for literary flourishes in the world of academic writing as well, and this book gives space to that potential elsewhere (see Chapter 6). For the moment, my focus is on the production of sentences and the use of our own resources therein.

What I want to highlight by using the term process is the notion of this being something dynamic, moving, ever changing. This can be conceptualised as a movement through various phases, through the contrasting corridors of our labyrinth, for instance. Or we can think of it as riding a wave of creativity which takes on different characteristics at different junctures. I do not wish to suggest that this creative process is a straight, unbending, fixed line. I would see it more as a cycle which has a tendency to spiral, sometimes taking us back to where we — almost but not quite — started, before we connect with the next — subtly altered — turn of the circle.

It is also a process personal to the individual. I am going to detail some stages below which may or may not sound familiar. They are there not to be accepted verbatim, rather to be looked on as giving pointers towards the elements of your own creative process. Is there something here which echoes with your own experience? If so, do you try to ignore it or even become irritated by it? Would knowing it is part of a process, a dynamic movement which will eventually bring you closer to your goal, make it easier to tolerate?

Summary Box

The creative process is about being resourceful, inventive and productive.
The creative process is a spiralling, dynamic movement.
The creative process is personal to the individual.

THE "CREATIVE PROCESS"

I have drawn on a number of influences (Moustakas, 1990; Barber, 2002; Kronsky, 1979; Angwin, 2003) in order to conceptualise the steps in the creative process. It owes much to the Gestalt Cycle and I have included an explanation of this in an appendix for those who wish to know more.

I don't want to depict a direct sequence, one thing rigidly following the other; more a cycling or a spiralling one which allows for much twisting round and doubling back. The creative process is active and rhisomatic; in other words, it is constantly on the move and we can find our way into it from many different entry points. The boundaries between the stages are indistinct and provisional. We will all have our own version and some of the steps proffered below will be more familiar than others. It is interesting to note this. However, it is also useful to consider whether the steps we are less comfortable with, which we feel like rejecting out of hand, do have something to offer us. Are we, by ignoring them, short-circuiting our own creative process?

"The Idea": Initiation, Connection and Reconnection

This is the kernel of an idea. This might be a long-held interest which we suddenly have the opportunity to investigate further. We might be given it, for example in the form of an essay title. We might need to go looking for it, as we have to come up

CHAPTER 1

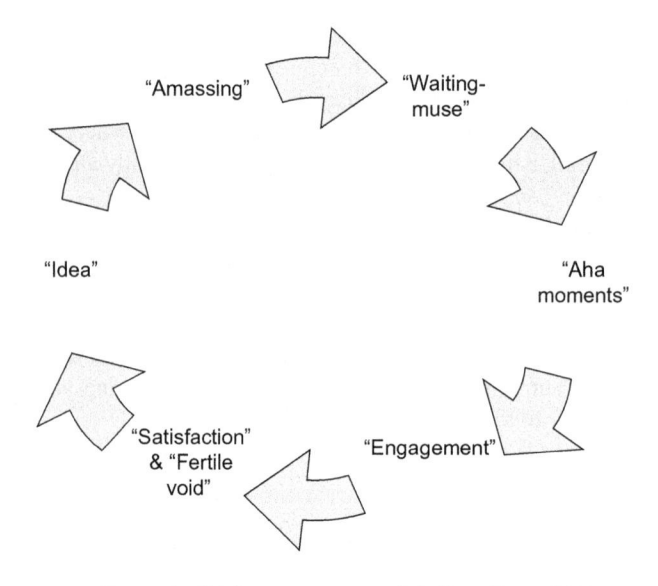

Figure 1. The "creative process" © Kate Evans 2012

with an area of research for our thesis or for a project. Or it might suddenly come to us, unbidden, apparently out of thin air.

For instance, since my teenage years I'd wanted to write a book. I always had lots of ideas for novels and also for non-fiction. I have published short stories and articles, and produced manuscripts which are book length. However, the idea for this book was not something I came up with. I was asked to review the extant literature on writing blocks for an edition of a journal looking at research being carried out by therapists. The rationale for my literature review was that therapists were being put off doing and presenting research because of writing blocks. I had written about writing before but not with this focus. I was intrigued by what I was discovering and encouraged by the responses I had to my article. A fairly routine task I had been given was beginning to take on a further potential; it was taking the shape of a book.

On the other hand, Mark (Case Study 1) struggles with essay titles he has been set. The "idea" is something he has to find an interest in and it is not always easy. Mark describes not being able to connect with essays which are "rehashings" of books he has read and other people's concepts, which he feels are distant from his own personal development. He expresses disinterest and finds it hard to get on with the writing.

By whatever means we acquire this embryonic idea, it is something which we're attracted to or which we have to find an attraction in. It niggles, pushes, begins to

12

demand attention. We may try to ignore it, but it will keep calling us back. At this time, it may be difficult to pin down or describe coherently; it may feel ephemeral. Do we feel irritated by it? Do we feel we don't have time for it now? Or perhaps we feel deskilled, not trusting our capacity to deal with the work involved? Feeling uncomfortable or downright antagonistic towards the idea is more likely if it is something, such as an assignment, which we are not pursuing by choice. Or we feel negatively about the course or tutor. Still, it is an emerging idea. And at some point, for the creative process to begin to roll we will have to connect with it. Perhaps looking beyond this particular piece of work to the greater goal of a complete course or qualification will help when relating with the idea is particularly difficult. The adage, "It doesn't have to be perfect, it does have to be done," might force a rusty creative process into motion. Or some of the loosening-up writing exercises at the end of this chapter may be effective.

Our connection with our embryonic idea could be intense, staying tight and sure. On the other hand, it might be faltering and insecure, especially if we are hedged in by doubts or are feeling bored or challenged. We may need to work hard to get hold of this idea at all and may have to keep going back to it to renew any enthusiasm we feel for it. Whatever we feel about the idea, the initiation of our creative process, it is likely that we will have to return to what started us off at points to reconnect, to find a new boost to what we are doing. Given that in our creative process we are likely to spiral round, almost, but not quite, returning to points we have previously visited, this reconnection might be with a slightly different aspect of the original inspiration that got us going.

"Amassing"

Once we have entered into our creative process labyrinth we begin to amass trappings and baggage. This is bound to include reading — lecture notes, books, journals — and doing some kind of review of what has already been written on the subject; scouring the internet, TV and radio; along with talking and listening to others. We may decide to be more strategic in our gathering, through, for example, research and data collection such as interviews and protocols, such as I did for this book.

Wright Mills (1959, pp. 196–7) advises, "Keep a journal" where "… you will not be afraid to use your experience and relate it directly to various work in progress. … It also encourages you to capture 'fringe-thoughts': various ideas which may be by-products of everyday life, snatches of conversation overheard on the street, or, for that matter, dreams. Once noted, these may lead to more systematic thinking, as well as lend intellectual relevance to more directed experience. … By keeping an adequate file and thus developing self-reflective habits, you learn how to keep your inner world awake. … The file also helps you build up the habit of writing." I return to the writing journal at the end of this chapter.

CHAPTER 1

Fiction writer Joanna Trollope (2003) describes amassing as creating a "gerbil's nest":

> Once the idea has settled itself in my consciousness, I start collecting relevant things. In stiff-covered, spiral-backed notebooks, I paste scraps of newsprint — remarks from interviews, quotations, photographs. I might add snatches of poetry, things I remember people saying, things I hear them saying now, ideas for scenes and situations. There's no order at this stage, but, oddly, a kind of sequence and series of emphases seem to emerge, as if a storyline is beginning to heave its way to the surface, through all the flotsam and jetsam.

At this stage it may not always be possible to be certain what are "relevant things", and some of the things collected will grow in relevance, while others will decline. This phase, then, requires an openness, an acceptance that the relevance of something may not be initially apparent and an eclecticism which might be unsettling (especially as the material mounts up) or counter-intuitive. Do you criticise yourself for spending an hour surfing the net because the number of words you actually note down are few? Or are you critical of the thirty minutes turning the essay question over in your mind, trying to see it from all angles, because all you come up with is a stray memory of a past family holiday, which can't be significant, can it? Do you give yourself credit for "amassing"?

As already stated, the creative process is rhisomatic, so we may enter it at different stages. For some people the amassing is ongoing and can be a method by which the idea is found. The writing journal (see later in this chapter) is a continuous amassing and can

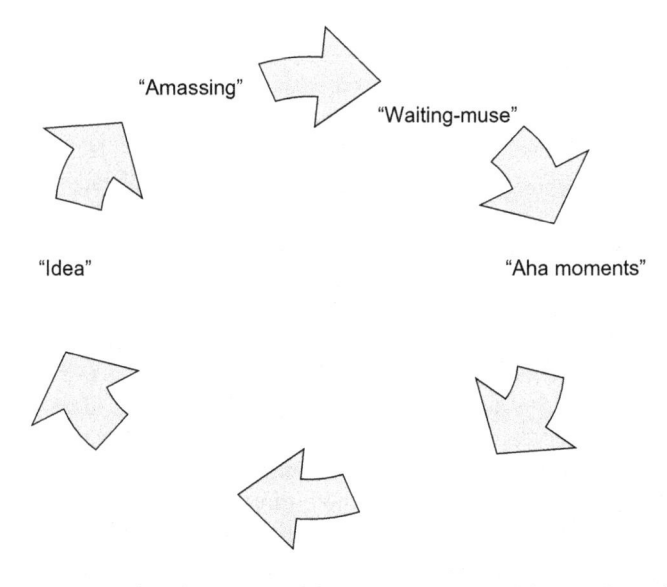

Figure 2. The first four stages of the "creative process" © *Kate Evans 2012*

be a source of many an insight which had looked dull and unusable when first gathered up and then flashes bright on a subsequent reading. For this book I had imagined I would complete the amassing stage and then complete a first draft which I would later rework. However, my amassing has run alongside my drafting and redrafting. This is partly the logistics of organising interviews, but also because the drafting and the amassing are feeding one into the other, opening up new areas for exploration, further questions. My amassing is a physical collecting of articles, notes, transcripts and other material into folders. It is also a writing journal where I can allow connections to present themselves. Early on I wrote: "I want another term for writer's block. The very term is self-defeating and self-perpetuating. Writer's permission. Writer's guide. Writer's map. I am a fan of cartography. I wonder if this is a good place to start for a metaphor. I am writing a book on writer's block — plotting a course. I notice my first act has been to clear a space. Create a file. A space which can now be filled."

The "Waiting-Muse"

We have taken up our initial "idea" and we have begun "amassing", collecting some of what we need. We stand on another threshold which might lead us deeper or lead us away. We watch, we tend, we sit for a while.

Phenomenological psychologist Moustakas (1990, p. 24) talks about "indwelling", the "turning inward to seek a deeper, more extended comprehension of the nature or meaning of a quality or theme of human experience." In some senses we are waiting, yet it is not an inactive, lethargic waiting. We are attentive, something is going on in us; but it is below the surface, we are not fully aware of it, at times it appears to be not of our own volition. It is, perhaps, our unconscious doing its stuff. As Robson (2010, p. 31) puts it, there is support for:

> [The] view emerging from several disparate fields of neuroscience — that the subconscious mind has a bigger role than previously supposed. When it comes to the mental faculties we prize as uniquely human, including creativity, language and aspects of memory and learning, subconscious thought processes are far from playing second fiddle to the conscious mind.

I have called it the "waiting-muse"; we are mulling over, ruminating, while we are attentive to the first stirrings of what we might be heading towards. We do not want to rush in and yet we do not want to leave. As with the Greek Muses before it, our waiting-muse is playing its role in the creative process.

Psychologist Jaynes (1990, p. 46) says, "We have been brought to the conclusion that consciousness is not what we generally think it is. ... It is not involved in the performance of skills and often hinders their execution. ... and indeed some of the most difficult instances of creative reasoning go on without any attending consciousness."

What is happening behind our most accessible thoughts is where the action is. And once primed the waiting-muse will continue to whirr away in the background,

CHAPTER 1

making connections, dreaming up new perspectives and different ways into the issue that we are examining. That's if we allow it to, are attentive without being impatient and are offering nourishment (continuing amassing) without insisting it produce.

I discovered while talking to a friend that she thought when I said I had a writing day I wrote continuously for seven, eight hours. This is rarely the case. Breaks are important to my own creative process, to allow my waiting-muse to take over. I often swim or walk during these breaks and almost always realise something new about what I am writing while I do so. Novelist Michael Morpurgo once described walking the lanes of Devon "dreaming" stories in his head and waiting "till the moment I think they are ready to hatch" before returning home to write them.

"Aha Moments"

Suddenly we see or feel something, an unexpected illumination, a clarity of thought or image which we've not had before. We have been amassing and allowing the waiting-muse to do its stuff and then, yes, it comes to us what we should be writing. The trigger may apparently come from an external source — perhaps something someone says or something we read — or from within us, maybe when we least expect it, as we wake from sleep or as we remember one of our dreams or as we do the washing-up. A question or an idea we've been struggling with glows with meaning and possibilities. We are fired up and excited. All the grim grind of grubbing around in the dark has been worthwhile. We have lit our way forward so that we know our path with greater certainty.

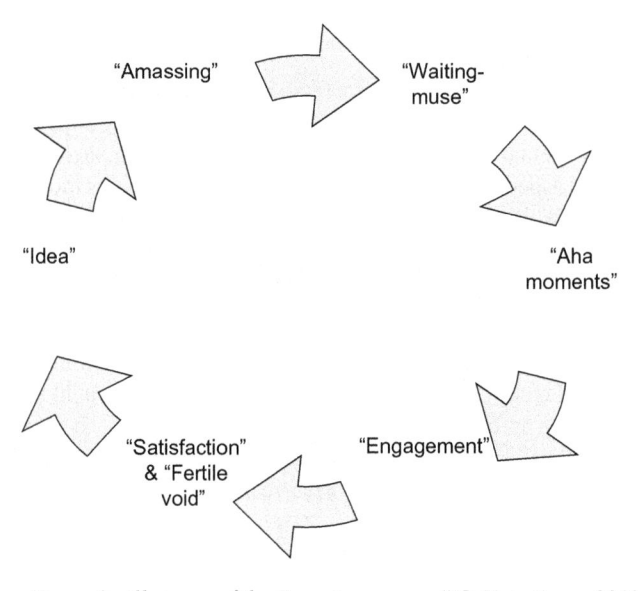

Figure 3. All stages of the "creative process" © *Kate Evans 2012*

"Engagement"

We are stoked and rolling. We are in a comfortable rhythm, the words are presenting themselves easily, we move between writing, picking what we need from our store and reflecting. We feel that we are moving on with our project. We are fully connected to what we are doing without feeling overwhelmed or taken over by it. As French author and Nobel Prize winner Andre Gide (Olsen, 1978, p. 156) says:

> One sentence follows another, is born of the other, and I feel as I see it being born and growing within me an almost physical rapture. This artesian welling up is the result of my long subconscious preparation.

At the moment, we are still talking about the creative process which brings forth the first draft. So though we are writing often (though not always) fervently and with relish, it is still messy and will have an unfinished, incomplete texture to it. I find this is a good point to seek feedback and encouragement, from people who are happy to respond to something which is still only half-baked. I say more about the importance of feedback — when and what kind is useful — in Chapter 5. Suffice to say here that a healthy creative process requires the input of others to maintain its momentum.

With this creative process we have the ingredients which we are beginning to mix together. We may have to go round the creative process a few times before we have the correct quantity of wobbly batter to fit into the cake tin. Then we can go for the baking, the rewriting and the editing of our piece. Editing generally looks at: syntax, the way we construct our sentences and paragraphs and how they flow; the overall construction of the work; and whether it says what we want it to say and speaks to the audience we are aiming at. The focus is not necessarily on spelling or punctuation (this comes into proofreading, which is the very last act and is best done by someone else if at all possible). Without wanting to confuse, I will say that rewriting and editing are also creative, like having the pieces for a patchwork and deciding on their shape, size and how they will come together. We have to have feedback to help us to do this, which may mean challenging what we are saying or how we are saying it. We may need to let go of our most treasured phrases and notions. We might need to think round problems and questions we had not initially thought of. This takes creativity. Rewriting and editing can dip back into the stages of the creative process, perhaps the amassing or the waiting-muse or there might be a few more aha moments, even though the focus is on fitting what we have into the dish we are preparing rather than mixing a new batter.

"Satisfaction" and the "Fertile Void"

I have taken the idea for these last two phases from the Gestalt Cycle (Clarkson, 1989). The penultimate phase is "satisfaction". Clarkson (1989, p. 35) describes this as "the 'afterglow' following full and complete experiences of intimacy or creative expression. ... This is the quiet after the storm..." We have completed what we set out to do; we feel the satisfaction of what we have done.

CHAPTER 1

The German word "Gestalt" holds within its meaning the idea of something completed, something whole. However, Clarkson (1989, p. 35) posits that the satisfaction phase "is frequently omitted from theoretical discussions of the [Gestalt] cycle. This may be a reflection of the lack of importance sometimes accorded to the closing phases of human experiences." And all too often we do not allow ourselves to feel satisfaction in our writing, be satiated by what we have done. We do not take the time to say "well done" — or seek others who will say "well done" on our behalf. Perhaps doing so seems arrogant or silly or can bring us in touch with our shame (see Chapter 2). We do not give a moment's thought to how far we have come, and only berate ourselves for not being further along. Or we go from our finished product to finding fault with it in one swift move. Satisfaction, however, is an important part of the creative process: it allows us to keep encouraged and motivated. For example, after four days writing undisturbed on this book, I wrote in my writing journal: "Gosh, feels like I am cooking on gas! I've got a lot done this week and I'm v. pleased with it. Well done, Katie!"

After satisfaction comes the "fertile void". There is a need for withdrawal, to rest and recuperate — for re-create-tion. This is not an empty phase. We are preparing for reconnection with our creative process. Much may be going on behind conscious thought, but what we are aware of is the need to take time out, perhaps do something completely different from writing. Clarkson (1989, p. 31) quotes Hall (1977, p. 53): "This state is pregnant with the limitless range of potential developments for the fully alive person. 'What interesting thing might happen next?' is the quiet, confident, open poised question."

The satisfaction and fertile void phases do not only come when a project is completed. They may come at the end of a day writing, a week spent on a particular topic, when the literature has been reviewed or a draft done. Breaking a writing-research project into manageable steps (chunking) is always a good plan. If we are aware of our need for satisfaction and fertile void phases we can use them to work out what size these steps need to be for us individually. In Case Study 4, Sarah is struggling with an article after completing the herculean task of her PhD literature-review chapter. As I reflected on our interview, it did occur to me that perhaps she had jumped her satisfaction and fertile void phases. Was she pushing on with the next task before she had acknowledged and digested the last? The pressure to do this will undoubtedly come from within and without. "A writer writes," is something I often say. All we have to justify our claim that we write is the words on the page. Though I should learn to modify this, for a writer also sometimes sits and contemplates or looks back at what they have done and says, "You know that's not half bad."

Writing — the Golden Thread

Writing can be the golden thread which leads us into and out of our labyrinth — our creative process. It can be the mechanism which ties the creative process together. It may not work for everyone; however, it offers potential for moving us through our creative process and working out where the brakes come on.

> **Case Study 3**
>
> Every day I was writing a diary and writing down what's on my mind, even just writing how difficult it is. I found that really useful. ... I know I can get back to it because sometimes I feel there's too much in there [my head] almost, and writing it down means it's there to go back to. ... I think through writing. It helps me to think through something and make sense of it. It's not just writing to get the ideas out but it can help to generate new ideas.

We can write to discover our "idea" and our "aha moments". Our own writing (and others') will be part of our "amassing" phase. It may retain our connection with our project during the "waiting-muse", though for some the "waiting-muse" takes the form of internal ruminating or dialoguing with others. At all these junctures, I am advocating a relatively free writing (see later in this chapter), an approach which is not to a rigid plan and is not afraid to go off-piste, to explore, to welcome in the unexpected. "Engagement" is perhaps the phase which will involve more structured writing; this will be the phase where the writing takes some (but not too much) account of audience, intention and assessment criteria. It's a good idea to write down the positive feedback we receive from ourselves and from others in order to be able to go back to it. This will deepen "satisfaction" and mean we can hold on to it more fully.

Even in the "fertile void" writing may have its place. Though not for all, a complete break from writing may also be good. A different genre of writing — poetry, fiction — or another genre of creativity — visual art, music, gardening — would be called for in the fertile void. To start to become more productive in terms of writing, giving our creative process regular care and practice does no harm. Just as taking a total break from going to the gym can make going back more difficult, leaving our creative muscles to go weak will make the return more painful. As with exercise, creativity can be folded into our lifestyle on a little-and-often basis (see the writing journal section later in this chapter), and this is an effective and health-giving attitude to being industrious and fruitful.

In describing this creative process in stages, I am aware that I am giving the impression that this is a slow, evolving journey. This could, no doubt, be frustrating for those who have only a week to complete what they are doing. On the other hand, people who are more familiar with their creative process and are aware of its own individual workings do tend to be more prolific writers and are able to regulate the creative process according to the needs of the piece they are producing. For instance, if I have a thousand-word article to write on something I am informed about, I can spend less time at each stage of the creative process than I am for this book and still come out with a piece which will meet the requirements of the journal editor and audience.

CHAPTER 1

> **Summary Box**
>
> The creative process has stages.
> Recognising these stages and working with them will make us more productive.
> The stages can be tailored to the length and depth required by the end product.
> Caring about and stoking our own personal creative process will mean we write more easily and can be folded into a little-and-often routine.

THE "CREATIVE APPROACH"

The force that through the green fuse drives the flower. (Thomas, 1988, p. 13.)

Inspired by others before me, I have attempted to conceptualise a creative process and present it above. However, research into creativity has mainly focused on whether we can define and analyse what I'm calling a "creative approach" (Phillips, 2005). There was research in the 1970s by Paul Torrance (Torrance, 1995), by Colin Martindale, a psychologist from the University of Maine (Phillips, 2005) and more recently by Guy Claxton at the University of Bristol and the University of Winchester (Claxton, 2012), among others. These studies have suggested that to be creative what is needed is "an attraction to complexity and an ability to handle conflict. [People who are creative] are also usually highly self-motivated, perhaps even a little obsessive" and have a "mental flexibility" which means they can "shift gear" easily between different kinds of thinking: for instance, between being intuitive, being evaluative and undertaking analysis (Phillips, 2005).

Psychologist Csikszentmihalyi (1996), and clinical professor of psychiatry Rothenberg (1990), also emphasise the capacity to be able to hold on to and work with divergent thinking — ideas, thoughts, feelings which appear to be contradictory or unconnected. And having an acceptance of the chaos out of which creativity flourishes (Nurse, 2012). At least part of this "chaos" is about allowing the unconscious to seep through. The idea of the unconscious mind has many attendant connotations; what I'm interested in are the flashes of inspiration, memories, notions, feelings which come from the part of the brain which is less boundaried, and less concerned, by received rules and the perceived judgements of others.

Writing is a "flow" activity as defined by Csikszentmihalyi (2012); it can become "spontaneous" and "automatic", it seems to take us out of "real" time. The hours pass without us noticing them. Our focus is on the words; we are carried away by the "flow" of them. This is akin to what I call the "joy of writing" (see Chapter 6).

Of course, when we are stumped and mired in a writing block, it is difficult to imagine being motivated or being open to a creative approach or being gripped by the "flow" of words ever again. These things are so far from our present experience as to feel like they are on another planet. However, it is possible to unpack the creative approach and find ways in, step by step. Ways of unblocking a creative approach are discussed in the writing strategies section below.

> **Summary Box**
>
> A creative approach — characterised by motivation, flexible thinking and tolerance of "chaos" — harnessed to experiencing writing as a "flow" activity can mean we write more fluently.

BLOCKS TO WRITING

By writing academically we engage our creativity; we engage in a creative process. Writing blocks may occur because we are not aware of our own individual creative process and we inadvertently hinder it from moving along.

Getting to know our creative process will allow us to see the patterns in our energy and appetite. At one moment we may be riding the rollers, and at another we may find ourselves becalmed. Each is important to the creative process: the rollers cannot exist without the becalming, and vice versa. Like an experienced surfer with the ocean, we can learn to judge the tides and currents of our creativity.

This can boil down to very practical observations, such as what time of day do we write best? I am a morning person. That's when I like to write. I can write later during the day, but I feel I am less vibrant, less energised. Others will write better at other times of day. If you are an evening writer then getting to your desk at 9am and "nailing" yourself there will do no good. You are fighting the natural flux of your creative process: not only will you find it tough to write, but feelings of failing and thoughts such as "I'm not getting this right" will compound your difficulties. A colleague I explained this to while she was writing a case study responded in an email, "I definitely work better after lunch, and evenings I peak! I have said that I am blocked at writing yet it might be that I am forcing myself to write at the wrong times for me." (Personal communication.) Are you finding yourself completely halted, merely because you think to be a writer you have to be a "lark" rather than an "owl"?

For all writers, however successful, the creative process is a dynamic one; we are not always in the engagement stage. Some phases, however, can bring their own anxieties if we are not cognisant of their attributes. For instance, amassing could bring the sense of being overwhelmed, of having too much material, of drowning in it.

> **Case Study 3**
>
> [There's] just too many ideas in there [my head], and floating about and [it's difficult] trying to cram everything into one article. ... I worry about losing something, missing something or forgetting about something. It feels quite chaotic at times...

The waiting-muse and the fertile void are phases of apparent inactivity, which can be hard to accept, especially if deadlines are looming. Yet by circumventing them, we risk becoming blocked because we don't have enough to say since we haven't given our creativity the opportunity to do its work below our conscious thought. Or we brand a crucial phase as a writing block, try to banish it and thereby undermine our capacity to produce and, furthermore, the possibility of generating innovatively. We are pathologising the normal ebb and flow of our creativity. Here, fiction and non-fiction writer Alan Garner describes a part of his creative process which I identify as a fertile void:

> I had had to be totally incapacitated in order to build the energy, to fill the reservoir, that would be needed. The analogy with an enforced hibernation fitted. If I could live with this self-loathing, and see it as a signal to let the waters rise, it could remain a necessary, though unpleasant, part of a positive and creative process. As long as that thought stayed, I could endure. (Garner, 1997, p. 212.)

As Garner indicates sometimes sticking with our creative process is not easy, with its twists and turns. We have to trust that even in doubling back we could be moving forward. We would rather take a short cut, round off the corners, be sure of what is coming and have our goal in sight. If we do not recognise our creative process or sense somehow it's "not right" then feelings of inadequacy and shame can come into play and these are the real paralysers (see also Chapter 2). They may induce us to jump too quickly to rewriting and editing, or even — the great blocker to the creative process — proofreading. This can bring us in touch with an assessing and judgemental audience quicker than is healthy for our creative process, thus stopping us from writing innovatively or writing at all. This is particularly true, perhaps, in an academic environment, where we feel that the audience could be especially critical and the formats we are writing to especially constraining.

Case Study 3

[When I'm] writing for an audience, I'm more aware of the fear, I mean the pressure of having to get it just right. ... Yes, I suppose it's having that need to be creative and then having to force it onto that narrow format [of the journal]. Yeah I suppose it's a mismatch there.

Furthermore, if we are troubled by how chaotic the early stages of our creative process might appear, then we can get stuck in constantly starting over.

Case Study 4

You keep on trying but I find a lot of the frustration builds up. It's a lot of effort and if you're constantly getting it wrong, which I tend to do, you get more flappy, a lot more flustered.

Getting "flappy" about the messiness may then spur us into editing and proofreading too early. Thoughts such as, "I'm not doing enough," or "This isn't good enough," may elicit feelings of incompetence which we then try to soothe by getting on with what can seem like the "proper job" of editing and proofreading. However, this is like trying to go forward in reverse gear. It's grating, it's unsatisfying, and, as such, it may stop us from writing entirely. The more unconscious, explorative phases — which I have named amassing and the waiting-muse — allow us to be open to the unlooked-for, the unexpected, the discovery, and accrue resources from our own perspective. Our own unique insight is more likely to surface if it is given the space and permission to do so. Without it we might grind to a halt.

While reflecting on Case Study 3, I was struck by the spirals I found there: for example, spiralling self-fulfilling prophecies to do with the fear of not finishing getting in the way of finishing. I am still left with the question: Was this part of a creative process? One that was difficult at times but could ultimately be productive? Each individual finds their own creative process; what I have done here is named some stages which I hope will enable you to do so. I have also suggested that what might be perceived as blocks to writing could, in fact, be aspects of a particular stage and knowing this, working with this, could be enough to free our writing hand again.

Writing is easier if we adopt a creative approach. Tolerating complexity, handling divergent thought, mental flexibility, motivation, "flow": these have all been found through research to be significant in a creative approach. They are also useful for scholarly activity, so are worth developing within academic environments. But you may feel all aspects of this creative approach is a lot to take on all at once, so pick one and focus on that. There are some pointers in the writing strategies below which may assist; since, in common with Csikszentmihalyi (1996) and Phillips (2005), I would suggest there are ways for us to enhance the factors which make up a creative approach for ourselves.

CHAPTER 1

> **Summary Box**
>
> The natural rhythms of the creative process may lead us to think that we are blocked.
>
> Certain phases of the creative process may cause anxiety because of their perceived chaos or inactivity.
>
> We can change our habits, sometimes only slightly, to work with, rather than against, our own personal creative ebb and flow.
>
> A creative approach can be fostered. It is already important to scholarly activity so, no doubt, you have the skills to develop.

WRITING STRATEGIES

The main message of this chapter has been to notice our creative process, work with it rather than against it and foster a creative approach. This may be a case of making slight alterations to our routine or being less impatient with ourselves when we are feeling the pressure to "get on with it". We could also begin to develop our writing through what I am calling an "academic writing apprenticeship". This encourages an attitude which will over time build competency and fluency. It fits in with the "little and often" stance which I mentioned before. A small amount of time given regularly to an academic writing apprenticeship now could save lots of wasted hours later tussling over a piece which has to be in for a deadline when we're feeling blocked and weary. I offer some ideas below. Even taking one of them on could make this difference. Before going on, if you have not already done so, please look at the "Read This First!" section in the introduction to this book.

The Academic Writing Apprenticeship

In some ways, writers are always "apprentices"; we are always becoming. There is always something new to discover. It is an adventure which can be exciting, frustrating and demanding by turns. In my experience, it requires some kind of relatively steady and regular commitment.

The academic writing apprentice:

– Looks out for models and mentors.
– Trains through projects appropriate to their skills level, working up towards the more challenging ones.
– Practises.

Reading is where the academic writing apprentice finds their models. This is not reading for content, for facts, for quotes, but reading for style. This might mean reading across disciplines (or even across genres, into fiction and poetry) to find a piece — an article, a review, a chapter in a book — which really engages you. Ask yourself: What is it about the writing which holds my attention? Is there one thing which this author does which I can bring into my own writing? Conversely, you could find a piece which bores you even though it is on a subject which interests you. Ask yourself: What is it about the writing which is dull and flat? How can I avoid doing this? You might like to find a colleague to discuss this with.

Reading books on writing is also a good way to get tips on style. There are, of course, books on writing academically which can help. But you can also dip into "how to" books looking at other genres such as novel or short story writing. Or read reviews in the literary sections of quality newspapers and magazines.

It is easy to get overwhelmed by advice. So look for one small thing which you personally feel you could implement easily and take that away to practise.

Mentors can come from a variety of places. We have tutors, supervisors, colleagues, peers, friends, friends of friends, relatives, relatives-of-friends; in amongst them will be people willing and able to become our writing mentors. We may be in contact with them face to face or online. They may be long-term mentors or recruited for a particular project. Perhaps they have specific technical knowledge appropriate to our discipline, or maybe they are voracious readers and are able to respond from that standpoint. They can give us encouragement to help our motivation, as well as precise feedback to help us move forwards. In our area we may find that there are academic writing groups or that we are able to instigate one. The point is to find a way of becoming a part of an academic writing community which is supportive and nurturing, even if it is only meeting with a colleague every couple of weeks over a coffee to talk about writing.

An apprenticeship requires that we work on the less complex, working up to the more challenging. Yes, we want to write that essay, article or book, but maybe writing that plan or summary or review or blog entry first will get us closer to it. It also requires that we let our drafts go before they are perfect to receive feedback from our mentors or supervisors or tutors. We accept that we make mistakes and we find people to be with us who are accepting of our mistakes, able to offer critical judgements which will help us to rectify what we have done rather than demolish us.

And finally, an apprentice practises. An apprentice academic writer — and in actuality we are all apprentices — writes regularly. Here are some tools which can assist with the practice of writing:

- The writing journal.
- Free writing.
- Taking a walk: embodied writing.
- Lists.

The writing journal   It is a truism which sounds rather banal, but writers are people who write. Talking about writing can definitely be useful. Reading — whether about writing or otherwise — is essential. But actually writing is a verb; it is in the doing that we connect with ourselves as writers and the writer within ourselves.

CHAPTER 1

Words are our medium; we have nothing else, so it is in the putting-down of words one after the other that we learn our craft. It sounds simple, yet, of course, it is not. Why else am I writing this book? If it were straightforward then there would be no writing blocks and we'd all be flourishing, prolific writers. However, in other ways it is beautifully simple. Writers need nothing more than words — a relatively common currency — to create. Most of us have command of a fair few words. If we can start by getting them down on paper, then we are on our way, we are becoming writers. If we want to run a marathon, we have to start taking those few painful running steps. If we want to become writers, we have to start putting the words we know down on paper.

> The arts of writing all begin in playing with words, wallowing in them, revelling in them, being obsessed by them, finding reality in them. Words are the mud this mudpie's made of. (Le Guinn, 2004, p. 60.)

Similarly, as with training to run a marathon for the first time, doing the activity regularly and with increasing earnestness is the way to increase our fortitude as a writer. We work up to writing the "big things" such as essays, articles, theses and books, by writing the small things, the brief descriptions or reflections, the musings, the letter, the book review. The first time we go for a run, we manage down the street before we get short of breath. If we persevere, then we find we are running further and further until the marathon finally seems a real possibility. And, of course, we will get setbacks. Days when we really don't feel like it, but go anyway. Days when we can't do what we are aiming for. Days when everything just seems to be going backwards. We can expect the same as we begin to flex and develop our writing muscles.

The practice of writing needs practice. Slow, plodding, regular practice which can seem dull. It can, however, take off and be playful and fun, especially if you are able to make friends with your writing, see it as a companion and also join a community of supportive writers who will travel alongside you.

How you begin and develop your practice of writing is up to you. I am suggesting a writing journal, also advocated by Wright Mills (1959) (see "Amassing" section page 13) and also described in Case Study 3. Here is a famous young diarist talking about hers:

> It's an odd idea for someone like me to keep a diary because it seems to me that neither I — nor for that matter anyone else — will be interested in the unbosoming of a thirteen-year-old schoolgirl. Still, what does that matter? I write, but more than that, I want to bring out all kinds of things that lie buried deep in my heart. ... "Paper has more patience than people." I thought of this saying on one of those days when I was feeling a little depressed and was sitting at home with my chin in my hands. ... I don't want to set down a series

of bald facts in a diary like most people do, but I want this diary itself to be my friend, and I shall call my friend Kitty. (Frank, 1997, pp. 6–7.)

My writing journal is fifteen centimetres by twenty. It has good-quality plain paper. It is sturdy and has a band which holds it closed. It is the right size for me to carry around, while still giving me the space to write loosely, chaotically, with abandon, if I want to. The lack of lines means I can choose my own spacing, wiggle my sentencing around, create shapes with words. For me there is something special about writing longhand onto paper; there is a greater freedom, I can write with less conscious thought, I can be more playful, get messier. There is a far greater chance that what I write will surprise me.

Your writing journal will be what you choose it to be. Perhaps it will be on a computer or some other electronic device because that is what works for you. However, I would urge you to try keeping a longhand journal for at least a short while, to see what the difference might be.

I like to use the word "journal", rather than "diary", because it shares the same etymological root as "journey". As such, it connects with the ideas of travelling through, of movement, of exploration. I use my diary for forward planning, knowing what I will be doing in an hour's, a day's, a week's time. It is about appointments and deadlines. My writing journal is about being in the moment or reflecting back. It is more expressive, more descriptive, more eclectic than my diary. The only aspect it shares with my diary is that each entry is dated. However, because the entries will vary in length and may not be strictly diurnal, a writing journal where the dates are already printed in would not work for me.

A writing journal is a "capacious holdall", as Virginia Woolf called hers. I might write about the events of the day and about how my writing is going. I will write about my feelings as well as my thoughts, I will write descriptively, I will allow my imagination to take flight. I will collect snippets of conversation or quotes from my reading or photographs or illustrations; or note anything that has caught my attention, raised a question for me, been a source of inspiration. I won't be too concerned about keeping things tidy or logical or in any kind of order. I won't worry at all about being perfect or right. I won't ask why I want to keep a record of whatever it is; I just will. I will accept that sometimes what I am doing is downloading and putting stuff down to get rid of it from my head and that this is unlikely to be useful to me when I reread it. Whereas some of what I write I will come back to and it will feed into the writing I do which is for sharing. And when I am writing in my journal, I will not know which is true of which entry.

The writing journal is not for sharing. It is a private space. It is a safe space. It is a place which no-one else can look into without express permission. It is a conversation I am having with myself and the ever-accepting page (Bolton, 1999). The conversation is on-going and need never be conclusive; it can allow for many and conflicting perspectives. What I write in the writing journal may become a springboard for writing which will be for an audience, but that is not on my mind as I write in it.

I write with no expectations, no aims, no plan, except to write, to put one word down after another. It will always be a place for the practice of my writing. When starting out, however, just as the novice runner finds each step painful, keeping a writing journal may feel more like a chore. Many things will get in the way of it. The blocks discussed in this book will come into play. Indeed, one of the first tasks of the writing journal might be to explore what makes it so difficult to keep going with it (perhaps using some of the exercises below). As with the runner, though there will always be days when it will feel like an impossible task, with commitment and regular application to it, keeping a writing journal will get easier. In my experience, it has become an essential part of my creative process, a storehouse of inspiration and a trusted companion.

Free writing Where to start with your writing journal? Where to start with your writing day? Where to start with your writing project? How to "warm up" before tackling that essay or dissertation chapter? One method I use is something I call "free" writing, though I have also heard it variously described as sprint, unconscious, unthinking writing. Earlier in this chapter I have discussed the role of the "unconscious" in creativity. Boden (2004, p. 29) says, "Creativity cannot be explained by conscious processes alone. Artists and scientists alike have argued that relevant mental processes must be going on unconsciously too." She quotes Picasso as saying: *"Je ne cherche pas, je trouve!"*

How do we put our own minds into a state where we are not searching but finding? Where we are allowing the unconscious processes to come out onto the paper? For me, "free" writing has been one of the answers. Goldberg (1986) gives the following "rules" for this "free" writing:

- Keep to a time limit*.
- Keep your hand moving.
- Don't cross out.
- Don't worry about spelling, punctuation, grammar.
- Lose control.
- Don't think. Don't get logical.
- Go for the jugular (if something comes up in your writing that is scary or naked, dive right into it. It probably has lots of energy).

* I would suggest initially three minutes, working up to five or ten.

The aim is to "burn through to first thoughts ... to the place where you are writing what your mind actually sees and feels, not what it thinks it should see or feel", to "explore the rugged edge of thought". (Goldberg, 1986, pp. 8–9.) This does take practice and may initially go against your writing instinct. But it is worth the effort. So let's have a go.

> **An Exercise in Free Writing**
>
> Starting with the words: "My creativity is…", write for three minutes (using Goldberg's rules). You may find it easier to use an alarm clock or kitchen timer to measure the three minutes, so you're not distracted by clock-watching.
>
> Scan what you have written (don't reread) and see what words come out at you. Highlight or circle three of them. Choose one to start off your next three-minute free writing. (You can choose the words at random, if none present themselves, by closing your eyes and letting your pen fall onto the page.)
>
> Repeat the scanning and highlighting and choosing of words before doing your final three minutes of free writing. If you scan and highlight three words from this last piece, then you should have about nine words to play with.
>
> And play is the operative word. Now you can have fun with these words and the title "My Creativity Is…"
>
> You can try the same exercise with: "My writing is…"; "My essay is…"; "My literature review is…"; "My thesis is…", for instance.

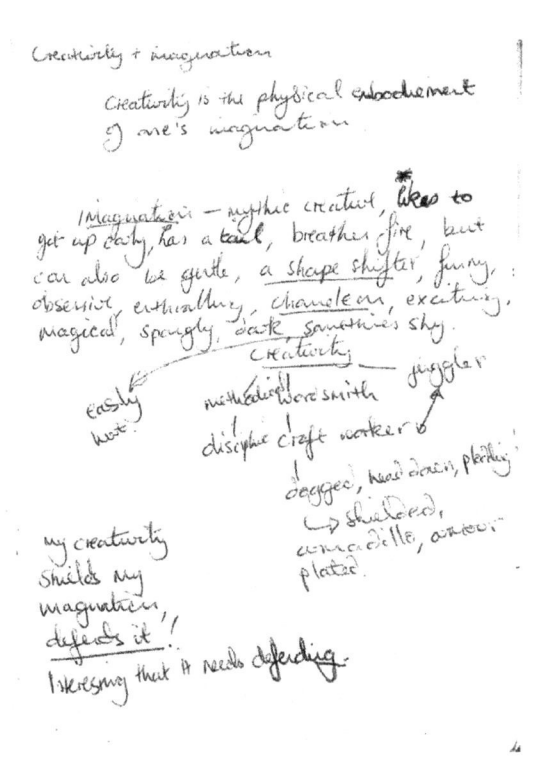

Figure 4. The messiness of free writing.

CHAPTER 1

In Evans 2011, my interviewee described free writing as "ploughing a field", going beneath "the now of the mind" and pulling things out. "It's almost like, aha, I knew it was there, I don't know why I didn't think of it before." He goes on to say that the act of writing down anchors and captures thoughts making them more available for consideration. Free writing, then, goes beyond talking and thinking, in that it reveals and then secures.

I have used quotation marks around the word "free", because it is free but within limits. The limits — usually in terms of time and often in terms of a subject or stimulus being a starting point — are important for making it less inhibited. They create boundaries, a place of safety, within which we dare to play, we dare to experiment, we dare to take risks, we dare to dream.

> Those who dream by day are cognizant of many things
> which escape those who dream only by night. (Edgar Allan Poe.)

Taking a walk: embodied writing Go for a walk, preferably on your own and preferably outside where there is some greenery. By turns, for maybe five minutes each, focus on noticing what you are hearing, then what textures there are about you, then what you are seeing and so on, until you have spent some time with each physical sense (sound, smell, touch, sight and taste). Focus on what is happening inside your body, then how it is interacting with the outside. When you have made this journey through your senses and your body, sit down and write for ten to fifteen minutes in your journal. Be as descriptive as you can and as specific in your descriptions as you can manage. You didn't just feel cold, but how cold? As cold as what?

Then scan through what you have written and pick out some words or lines which resonate with you. Form them into clusters with up to five lines. Here's one I wrote:

> Seagulls fold their wings
> drop into the sea
> like tennis bombs
> casually thrown and missed.
>
> Waves whirlygigg pebbles
> in a rush to applaud their own finish.
> Slap, slap, slip, slop
> across the sand in sequined sandals.
>
> Toddlers break the sky
> with their startling shouts,
> they know they are too small
> to fill the ocean
> so they scream themselves huge.

Once we start to focus on our senses and how our bodies are feeling or responding, we are beginning to practise "embodied" writing. Writing which is not only from the head, from our thoughts and our imagination, but is also informed by our body and mind working in concert. As suggested in Chapter 6, this brings in information which would otherwise be lost or disregarded. For example, I know that the uneasy feeling in my stomach I sometimes get when I sit down and write is about anxiety. If I focus on that uneasy feeling, words come to mind about "making a fool of myself" and "putting myself out there". My stomach told me about my anxiety, my head gave me some words for that anxiety.

On the other hand, sometimes I can get "locked" inside my head. Thoughts chase each other round and round and I feel overwhelmed and lose clarity. "Taking a walk", focusing on my physical senses, brings me out of my head and into my whole body. It allows me to escape from those circular ruminations which are often unhelpful.

We may find that we are more likely to lean towards one physical sense than another. For example, we may be more visual, whereas we find it difficult to remember or describe smells or textures. By paying attention to a sense we do not normally give much consideration to we can create a stronger description in our writing, a richer sense of what it is we are trying to communicate.

> **Writing Exercise: Embodied Writing**
>
> For one week become obsessed with a sense which you are not normally so aware of. Write each day for five minutes, focusing only on that sense. Try to be as specific as possible; for example, rather than, "The air felt damp," write, "The air felt damp as a… dishrag."

Using our senses in embodied writing can give us more information about how we feel about the academic writing we are doing and what may be getting in the way of us progressing.

> **Writing Exercise**
>
> Answer the following questions: What does my thesis/essay/article/review (delete or add to as necessary) taste like? What does it smell like? What colour is it? What shape? What does it weigh? What does it sound like? What texture does it have? Then scan through what you have written and pick out some words or lines which resonate with you. Form them into clusters with up to five lines.
>
> *Example*
> My book
> smells fragrant, of lilac on a cold bright morning;
> it tastes of mango,
> juicy and sweet.

CHAPTER 1

> **Writing Exercise (Continued)**
>
> My book
> is blazing red, smooth, a breathing pelt of a fox.
>
> Sometimes it is awkward to get hold of;
> I touch it and it falls apart or begins to grow amorphously.
> It is heavy, with the tonnage of a church bell
> and the force of a steam hammer.
>
> This expresses some of the mixed feelings I have in writing this book, the sweetness and also the concern that it will get out of my control, prove too much for me. Seeing this in words reminds me that I do need to seek support in order to manage it. The "fox" and the "breathing pelt" were a surprise until I wrote them down, and came from the words "red" and "smooth". The book is a breathing, living creature; it has cunning. I like this idea. On the other hand, it might also be a little scraggy at the edges and probably has fleas.

Lists Many of us make lists in our daily lives. They are often mundane and routine; yet they can also be a route in. Try to make the list as quickly as possible without thinking too critically about what you are writing down, and choose a high number of items for the list to aim for — like 37 or 60 or a 101. That way you are likely to push yourself beyond what's obvious (though don't worry if you don't make your target, that's not important). Allow yourself to put items down more than once, frequently it's what gets repeated which is important.

Making a list might be just a way of getting things out onto the paper which you will not immediately (or ever) decide to work with. On the other hand something surprising may appear which you want to explore further, perhaps an idea to take your studies forward or a question you will search out an answer to. Either way, don't be immediately dismissive of the list you've made. Allow it to remain as it is and perhaps come back to it at a later date.

Lists might start with: "37 things I know about.... myself as a writer"; "37 things I would like to know about.... my essay"; "37 things I dread... when I begin writing". Have a go at these for openers, but then come up with some for yourself.

This next list comes with inspiration from *The Poem that was Really a List* by Francesca Beard (2003). I took her repeating refrain and added my own ideas.

> The caretaker who is really a poet.
> The criminal who is really a protester.
> The civilian who may be a rebel.
> The child who is collateral damage.
> The terrorist who might have been a goatherder.
> The wrestle which was really an embrace.

The philosopher who was really stone.
The scaffold which was once a tree.
The meditation that was really sleep.
The words which became a knife.

How about starting yours: "The essay/article/thesis (delete as necessary) which was really…"?

Another list which is interesting to make is in answer to the question: What do I need to assist me to develop as an academic writer? This is a list I made during the writing of this book:

- Permission. Our own and permission from others to put the resources required into our writing.
- Time. We will certainly need time to devote to our writing, to honing our skills. This is time away from friends, family, other tasks we normally do. Perhaps this needs to be negotiated and delineated.
- Physical space conducive to how we write. For me this is a demarcated space, a room, where I have a computer and a rocking chair (where I sit to read or write longhand) and shelves for my books. It is quiet, I can close the door on the rest of the house. For you the physical space could be a different one. Perhaps you like writing in a library or a café or on the move in a train. There are downsides to this. For instance, a library may not always be open; in a café your need to write may not be taken seriously and friends may assume it is OK to interrupt you; if you are going to do all your writing on a train, it's going to get pretty expensive. However, it is useful to be aware of the environmental aspects which you find conducive to writing and you might be able to replicate some of them in a more accessible space: for example, the radio might give you the chatter you need. The point is to find a place which you're happy to write in and which you can access regularly, preferably on a daily basis.
- Psychological space is perhaps not so easy to mark out. Anxiety, pressure from others to do other things than writing, worries from the daily grind and so on. There always seems to be something better or more important to do than getting on with your writing practice. To counteract this may require continual reinforcement of your decision to put effort into your writing, both to yourself, as well as to those around you. This is something which is important to you and of value and, therefore, worth the effort. You may find that some of the anxiety and worries come out in the writing you do in your writing journal, and you may also choose to tackle them through talking to others: supportive friends, for instance, or colleagues or health and other professionals. The emotional aspects to writing blocks are important and sometimes more hidden than the more practical ones (see also Chapter 2) so they are worth considering in one way or another.
- Grieving. Making a commitment to writing will probably mean letting go of something else. If we make time and space for it in our lives then fairly inevitably

something has to give somewhere else. It is important to acknowledge this and make the decision consciously and thoughtfully. There may be other griefs that are less obvious which might still undermine our purpose, such as our concept of ourselves having to be altered or the fact that someone we wanted to see us achieving at writing is no longer around. There is little that can be done about grief, apart from acknowledge it, express it and seek support until it has run its course. However, grief left unresponded to can be destabilising.

- Acceptance of ourselves as someone who can write. For some there will be a strong sense of being an "imposter" (Huston, 1998. See also Chapter 2) or a fraud, which will make it difficult to value what we are doing enough to claim the space and time for our apprenticeship. Sometimes it is a question of faking it till we make it, taking on the mantle of writer before it really fits, until we can alter it sufficiently to our contours.
- Cheerleaders and critical friends. A community of fellow travellers and writers who are able to offer by turns encouragement, support and feedback which you can trust and moves you forwards.

This is my list. I invite you to make your own. Does this already identify something that is missing? Something that is getting in the way of your writing? Perhaps it is something practical and a slight alteration of your routine or your living space could answer it. Maybe it is more emotional and just acknowledging it is enough for it to become less weighty, allowing you to feel less hindered in your writing.

Summary Box

Becoming an "academic writing apprentice" can help us unblock our creative process and creative approach. Look out for examples of good writing to emulate and for supportive mentors.

Writing little and often trains us up to be more comfortable with the longer, more complex writing tasks of essays and theses. Use a writing journal for as little as fifteen minutes every other day to develop and perk up flagging writing muscles.

CONCLUSION — OUR OWN PERSONAL CREATIVE LABYRINTH

I have described the stages in a "creative process" which is iterative and rhisomatic, in other words, it spirals, feeding into itself and can be accessed at any number of points. I have explored the aspects of a "creative approach" with its tolerance of complexity and divergent thinking, of "chaos" and its connection with motivation and "flow". I have looked at what may block our writing in terms of the mechanisms of the creative process. I have offered a "little and often" writing strategy which might unblock both our creative process and approach.

We all have our own individual versions of the creative process and the creative approach. It is in getting to know our own and accepting them, working with them rather than against them, that we begin to open up our writing potential.

> [Creative people] may spend two hours at their desk then go for a walk, because they know that pattern works for them, **and they don't feel guilty.** (Phillips, 2005, p. 42. My emphasis.)

Entering the corridors of our own personal creative labyrinth for the first time can be unsettling; we are uncertain of what is to come and what we may find. However, the more familiar we become with the journey into the centre and back out again, the less trepidation we will feel. We will know that there will be corners which we find tough to negotiate, glitches that we forget about until the next time we face them, as well as places where we can relax and dream and others where the journey seems to take on its own comfortable momentum. The labyrinth becomes ours for us to explore and profit from. And through using our writing in different ways we set down our own golden thread, which is our security that we will work our way through the different passages; our golden thread, which becomes more robust the more times we retrace our steps.

CHAPTER 2

HAZARDOUS GROUND

The Relational and Emotional Aspects of Writing Blocks within the Academic Environment

This is the spot on the map where a quagmire is indicated, along with, "There be dragons" scrawled in red. And yet we cannot avoid this region: to arrive at our destination we have to go through it. Indeed, we may have reached this point many times before and retreated or tried to go round, though we always come back to it. Maybe we'll sit for a while on a lichen-covered rock and contemplate the seemingly firm ground in front of us, listening out for the heated breath of the monsters which lurk. Perhaps if we can only go quickly enough, tripping lightly from tussock to tussock, we will get to the other side without disturbing those mythic creatures. Somewhere deep inside, however, we know that we will slip, our boots will be sucked into the marshy ground and we will be held imprisoned, as the heavy pad of dragon foot and weighty swish of dragon tail come ever closer.

INTRODUCTION

Writing is a relational activity. When we write we are communicating. Initially we will be communicating with ourselves as we are our own first readers. However, even as we read through our initial draft, it seems to us as if there are other people crowding round us. These other people may be real or imagined, from our past, our present or our future. They can inspire us to keep going or close us down. This very relationality means that when writing we feel that we are revealing parts of our selves. This revelatory sense coming from the act of writing has an emotional impact which can stymie us. It can raise our own personal dragons from the deep. And yet I also want to say that this need not be so. The relationality of writing offers us the possibility of being heard and understood in all our complexities and wonder. It is, therefore, what can draw us on. The dragons can turn out to be gentle creatures, their fire warming not burning; the mire could be a sweet-tasting source for wild flowers.

In this chapter I want to explore:

– The relationality of writing.
– The consequent emotional impact.
– How relationality and the attendant affective domain can stop us writing.
– Writing strategies which can tame our personal dragons.

CHAPTER 2

THE RELATIONALITY OF WRITING

We are never alone in our writing. We may be physically the only person in the room facing the blank page or computer screen, but when we write, or even think about writing, other people gather. The impulse to write is the impulse to communicate something to somebody. The initial communication is likely to be with our self, as we become the first reader of our own words. Then comes the contact with other audiences — imagined, expected, potential and actual. It is through communication that we encounter and interact with our self and with other people.

> [Writing] lies at the moment of encounter: we meet our truth and we meet ourselves; we meet ourselves and we meet our self-expression ... (Cameron, 1993, p. 82).

As humans we are hard-wired to be relational. Current research suggests, "not only that human behaviour is fuelled by relational concerns, but also that the human psyche is fundamentally relational in nature." (Cashdan, 1988, p. 23.) We seek out and reach towards other humans as a matter of course and in writing we are no different. We want to make contact; we want to be understood.

In any communication there is a transaction. This deal goes something like: I will deliver meaning in a form (often predetermined by "rules" known to both of us) using signs (letters/words) which you, the receiver, are prepared to accept, or, at least, tolerate, and work with (Gergen, accessed 29th May 2012). In the pact formed in academic writing, we are using a relatively common currency, the written word, and yet this apparently simple transaction is complicated by the academic conventions which have to be learned and may be more implicit than explicit (see also Chapter 5). In addition, writing has a permanency which gives it a weight; perhaps even more so in the academic environment, where we are often being assessed or judged through our writing. There is a tension being built up in this transaction, therefore, between the ostensibly straightforward exchange of an everyday currency and the actual significance of the words we choose.

Facing Ourselves

Writing is a deeply personal and revealing experience. It can be like looking in a mirror, a powerful act of "self-intimacy" (Cameron, 1993, p. 20).

> [Writing] brings things to light. It illuminates us. It sheds light on our lingering darkness. It casts a beam into the heart of our darkness and says, "See?" (Cameron, 1993, p. 67.)

We reveal ourselves to ourselves in our writing; we may reveal aspects of ourselves which we are less aware of, parts of our "unconscious". This can be challenging; however, as we have seen in Chapter 1, the unconscious plays an important part in bringing forth the gems of thought and phrase which make our communication glow and engage. Cutting ourselves off from our unconscious can mean we begin to stutter and lose our flow of words. Nor is the unconscious necessarily that terrible to look at. As Jacques Derrida suggests, what may be felt to be "monstrous" is often not so once it is brought into the light and can be seen clearly (Hunt, 2007). For poet Seamus Heaney, the "pool of yourself", the "unconscious", is what entices you back as a writer (Heaney, 1984).

> **Summary Box**
>
> Writing is inherently relational. Through it we reveal our selves to ourselves. The act of writing brings us into contact with audiences — real or imagined, from our past, our present or our future. We enter into a transaction where we offer something to another in the hope of being received and comprehended. The academic transaction is perhaps more weighty than it at first appears because of the conventions which are embedded in it.

THE EMOTIONAL IMPACT OF WRITING'S RELATIONALITY

Even as I type this I can feel my own anxiety growing. This is not only between me and the computer screen — there are others involved. The relationship between writer and audience is a "thickly populated" one (DeYoung, 2003, p. 2), with the real and imagined attitudes and expectations of people (absent and present) playing a pivotal role. We seek and desire relationship and it is our experience of these both past and present which moulds, in one way or another, not only our approach to others and our anticipation of how they will react, but also our sense of what we are capable of. As Cashdan (1988, p. 23) puts it: "To understand what motivates people and how they view themselves, one needs to understand how relationships are internalised and how they become transformed into a sense of self."

Our first reader — our self — then, is likely to have imbibed through the years the critical comments carelessly (or not so carelessly) thrown out by parent/teacher/friend/peer/colleague/relative/employer/employee/student (subtract or add as necessary). How often do we write something only to hit the delete key moments later, our first reader — our self — having delivered a damning critique?

In academia, however, we are most often writing for a wider audience than just one, some of whom we may know personally, others who are anonymous. And it is frequently the imagined, expected and potential crowd and comments, rather than the real and actual, which are the most destructive. The readers we have never met, and who may not in reality exist, are the ones with the sharpest teeth waiting for the writer to show vulnerability or lack of understanding or technique so they can tear into them. They know just the phrase or look (which we hear or see in our mind) to make us over-question ourselves. They are the ones who habitually stand around us as we type or write, smelling their prey.

CHAPTER 2

In Case Study 2, Sue talks about her "ghosts" who repeat what people have said to her in her past so that her writing is halted in her present. For instance, when doing her PhD, the phrase, "Don't get too big for your boots. Dr Sue? What're you thinking of?" arrested her progress.

As I began this book I noted in my writing journal[1]: "When I imagine myself as having authored a published book, there is a large, leaden shadow creeping over my achievement. It forms into the word: 'disappointment' and then into 'failure'. Where does this heavy-booted spectre at the banquet come from? Until I had a conversation with a friend, I had forgotten that my father had written a book. I don't remember the work he put into it — though it was substantial, by family accounts. I do remember, however, his disappointment afterwards. I got another blast of this when I spoke to him the other day. He remembers having to viciously edit down what he had written, that there was no second print run and what was left of the first run was pulped. His dissatisfaction and disillusionment were still palpable even after forty years." The "ghosts" can go a long way back into our past and our inherited past.

Our "ghosts" may be about self-preservation, a defence against the imagined/expected/potential mêlée of readers, cruel, red in fang and claw. If we don't write, if we leave the page blank, then there is nothing for them to feast upon, nothing for them to pull to pieces. Our writing — and ourselves — remain intact as they remain un-communicated and un-encountered. Again, I take from my writing journal early on in the writing of this book: "Yet on the day I set for starting off on my writing journey I was resistant. What is there to fear? 'Except failure,' said that cranky little voice. 'Define failure my cranky little voice,' I respond. 'If my aim is to write and I write to the best quality I can achieve at the time, then failure is impossible.' 'Exposure,' the voice screeches." Artist Tracey Emin said, "I put my head above the parapet, I expect people to take pot shots and that's what we humans."

The relationality of writing, then, creates a tension. There is the desire to reach out, to be heard, to encounter, coming up against the fear of that encounter. In that encounter we may be criticised, we may be misunderstood, we may not be met. On the other hand, and this could also be an anxiety, we may be understood only too well. Our vulnerabilities, the bits of ourselves which we normally keep hidden, might become apparent. Or we may prove to be more able than we thought possible. We may shine, receive praise. We may get noticed. In both Case Study 1, and Case Study 3, I detected an ambivalence underlying the stories of writing blocks. Mark said he used his writing block as a "weapon" to "blow" deadlines, to seize control, to get noticed He believed he would not be noticed for the academic work he was capable of turning in. Was he substituting getting noticed for the "wrong" reasons for the possibility of getting noticed for the "right" ones: a well written essay? Similarly, Sarah, undermined her attempts at finishing with fears of never being able to finish. Rather than being anxieties about not achieving, were these, in fact, fears of success? What would happen if they did complete, did hand in something noteworthy, were, indeed, distinguished by their work? A writing block may be about hiding trepidation about success as much as about being found wanting.

To communicate: to converse; to convey; to connect. The word "communication" implies we have something to say, that we have something that we want to put out there, that we want others to hear. Already the doubts are piling in: do I really? Do I believe in the veracity, the validity, the originality of this something? And, even if I do, do I also believe that I am the right person to say it? Do I have the right? And who ordains this right anyway? In any encounter there is the potential for interaction, for some kind of comeback. Our words will be tested out, probed, perhaps misunderstood and misconstrued. Maybe other people won't "get" what we mean, which might lead us to conclude that they don't "get" us, who we are.

Summary Box

The relationality of writing causes a tension: we want to reach out and be understood, but we are anxious about being seen by others. Stopping ourselves from writing is one way of resolving that tension.

The relationality of writing means we are surrounded by "ghosts" whose words are conjured up from real and imagined critiques. The words may be cutting and silencing. However, we may be trying to defend ourselves from potential disparagement or even potential praise.

WRITING BLOCKS — THE AFFECTIVE DOMAIN

> We all know from experience that writing involves a great deal of cognitive energy. But for most, if not all, people, writing is also an experience that involves strong feelings and emotions: pain, pleasure, frustration, enjoyment, angst, annoyance, relief and stress. The affective domain in writing is important and is therefore worth exploring and discussion, with the aim of helping people to recognise it, to "deal with it" and to improve their writing by doing so. (Wellington, 2010, p. 136.)

We have already seen how the relationality of writing has an emotional impact which may bring our writing to a halt. Now I want to explore further into the affective domain to uncover some of the feelings which could be at the core of our writing blocks. These feelings may be well hidden behind phrases such as, "I'm bored," or "I'm not bothered," or "I ran out of time." They may, therefore, require some unpeeling. A place to start would be in asking questions like: How would we characterise ourselves as a writer? How do we feel about our writing? How do we feel about the audience which is eventually going to receive it? I will now look at some of the emotional content at the centre of writing blocks under sections exploring:

– Shame.
– The critical review.
– Our writer self.

CHAPTER 2

Shame[2]

The stern Bard ceas'd, asham'd of his own song; enraged he swung
His harp aloft sounding, then dash'd its shining frame against
A ruin'd pillar in glittering fragments, silent he turn'd away,
And wander'd down among the vales of Kent in sick and drear lamentings.
(William Blake, *America — a prophecy*, 1793, Preludium)

For me it's a sinking feeling, a desire to fade away, disappear. We all have our own experience of shame, which may include a sense of wanting to blank ourselves out or to run away; perhaps of anger; or of being acutely aware of ourselves and our failings. I fear that just writing or reading this section may bring on the symptoms. I think what probably unites most experiences of shame is a paralysis, an inability to get on with the job in hand, which might manifest itself as a feeling of tedium or in the action of walking away. So maybe, dear reader, your fingers are already poised to turn this page, accompanied by the thought, I don't need to know about this.

Writing, however academic it might be, is inherently revealing of our selves; it is "exposing" (Quaytman, 1971, p. 56). We are holding up a part of who we are for public scrutiny and giving others (who may never have put their words on the line) the power to shoot us down. This is more frightening and potentially damaging if we have a lot to lose, for instance in terms of professional reputation, or if the subject matter is close to our hearts.

To be on show, and, therefore, open to the (supposed or real) judgement of others, also increases the potential for shame.

> To feel shame is to feel seen in a painfully diminished sense. This feeling of exposure constitutes an essential aspect of shame. Whether all eyes are upon me or only my own, I feel deficient in some vital way as a human being. And in the midst of shame, an urgent need to escape or hide may come upon us.
> (Kaufman, 1992, p. xxi.)

Kaufman (1992) and others (such as DeYoung, 2003; Yontef, 1993) suggest that shame is created through a process of negative re-enforcements during childhood. This becomes so internalised that the desperately painful feeling of self-consciousness, of wanting to evaporate, feels normal. By then, an individual will expect any notice given to them to be inevitably critical. Praise is not possible. And any offered will often be misinterpreted to fit with the shame imperative.

> After internalization, exposure itself takes on a much more devastating meaning. Exposure now means exposure of one's inherent defectiveness as a human being. To be seen is to be seen as irreparably and unspeakably bad.
> (Kaufman, 1992, p. 75.)

Kaufman (1992, p. 32) describes "our" (contemporary Anglo-American) culture as a "shame-based culture" created by the injunctions to succeed, be perfect, be popular and conform. "Being different from others becomes shameful. To avoid shame, one must avoid being different, or being seen as different. The awareness of difference itself translates into feeling lesser, deficient."

As we have already said, writing something down is being seen, it is making ourselves visible, literally in black on white. And, I would want to add, writing something meaningful, something that comes from what is uniquely our self, is risking revealing our difference.

In addition, the layers of shame — personal and that created by a "shame-based culture" — are likely to be more acutely felt by those who juggle identities which are categorised as, and/or are in actuality, minority and, therefore, perceived as "different", within the environments they are operating in (Phillips & Pugh, 2005, p. 112). A black person within a department which is predominantly white, for instance, or a woman in a faculty staffed overwhelmingly by men, or a student with disabilities in amongst an able-bodied class. The sense of difference for these people could increase the potential for shame to thwart their progress.

Writing, as opposed to other forms of communication, has an augmented capacity for inducing shame because of what Quaytman (1971, p. 56) calls a belief in the "irreversibility of the printed word". A written word appears to carry more weight than a spoken one; it is harder to erase or alter over time. It remains there on the page, even if we, the author, have moved on and changed our minds. The sense that we have to "get it right" if it is written down is increased, making it harder to put words on the page.

Johnstone (1983) picks up this theme and explores how the attendant blocks might appear in different guises:

> Like apprehension that one's writing is "never good enough", a guilty sense that one is appropriating an unearned authority may also diminish incentive and some confidence in some writers. ... A writing block prompted by apprehension or guilt may appear as "perfectionism" or "premature editing", or it may lead to avoiding writing altogether — procrastinating. The writer who fears he "doesn't know enough yet" may protect himself against fear of not knowing enough or having enough to say by drawing out preparations — taking more and more notes, for example — until a research project has so grown in scope that the writer feels inadequate to taking it on. (1983, pp. 159–160.)

Jones (1975, p. 415) also tackles procrastination caused by grandiosity and discounting:

> The grandiose expectations function as a "Be perfect" driver analogous to an automatic hydraulic lift which constantly raises demands. As long as the individual procrastinates, the vaguely described project grows. While the project multiplies itself, the potential writer feels smaller and smaller, i.e. he discounts his or her adequacy.

CHAPTER 2

Shame is an emotion that is created tier on tier and it can whirr away in the background without being clearly recognised, obscured by phrases such as, "There wasn't enough time," or, "I'm just not much of a writer." Shame is likely to play a greater role in academic writing, given that shame is likely to infiltrate many a learning experience through life and affect our view of our capabilities to learn (Noor, 2006).

> People develop an image of self as learner, which is influenced by parents, teachers and others in authority and that this image will either facilitate or impede the person's subsequent learning. (Gilbert & Evans, 2000, p. 57.)

Past experiences of learning shape present experiences, shape whether we see ourselves as capable learners, shape whether we are undermined by a sense of lack of capacity or by imagining being seen to do well.

A colleague who is pursuing an MA sat down and told me her dream. She is in a meeting with her supervisor and he begins to give her feedback. "For intellectual acuity," he says, "I give you one out of five." He carries on, "For commitment to your MA, I give you one out of five." And so on, down a list of assessment criteria which my colleague has no knowledge of. She listens, she is given no opportunity to respond or put her own case. All the while a small mob of tabby cats are scratching away at her legs and skirt. She woke up feeling unsettled and disturbed by the dream. However, she was able to identify it as representing ideas she had received in the past about her capacity to do academic work. When she had achieved previously in educational environments, her mother had given her the message that she was "getting too big for her boots" and that, in any case, she would "never amount to much". Her dream supervisor and the cats were these age-old negative injunctions intent on trying to drag her down and "put her in her place". They were being transposed onto her present educational experience, even though it is proving to be a very positive and successful one. It coincides with her daring to go for this higher-level qualification and to be high-flying.

Shame that paralyses our writing comes from the sense of being revealed, of being seen as different. It comes from negative assessments of ourselves becoming so familiar and internalised that they feel inevitable and indisputable. Shame can close us down immediately or push us to have such high expectations, putting the bar higher and higher, that we feel a failure even when we are capable and succeeding. Shame can lead us to fear failure, however, equally it can lead us to fear success, for with success comes being noticed, comes more exposure. In the end, it is the fear of being seen at all which stops us in our tracks, whether that is through not quite making the grade or through achievement.

The Critical Review

It is rare in the academic environment that we are writing just for ourselves, that we are writing something which won't eventually be put to an audience, an audience which judges. Our writing will be assessed, evaluated, it will be given a critical review. Inevitably there will be "points for further development", that is the point of academic appraisal, to suggest ways of improving what we are doing. Hopefully this will be mixed with praise and enthusiasm. Yet implicit in this feedback is the idea that something can be made better, and that, therefore, we are being criticised. It is interesting that in the thesaurus, "criticism" includes both "disapproval" and "appreciation", though this is not always remembered by reviewer or writer. Wellington (2010) identified "the emotional aspects of feedback" (p. 138) and "the fear of an audience" (p. 146) as common inhibitors to writing.

The peer review is one type of feedback peculiar to the academic environment which can be particularly blocking. The anonymous critiques which brook no discussion and can feel as if they are being handed down by some mythic Greek gods who toy with humankind according to their whim. Boice and Jones (1984, p. 571) observe that certain exclusionary factors in this reviewing and publishing procedure might put certain writers off, especially minority and female academicians, before they have even started. They go on to note particularly the "Matthew Effect (Matt. 25:29 'For unto everyone that hath, more shall be given…') or the tendency for those who are already established to reap more citations and recognition from others who publish associated work." This system gives the novice the sense that there is a closed circle which they cannot break into and to which they have nothing to contribute. It has the potential for stilling people's pens even before they have begun, akin to Foucault's "gaze" (1974):

> We are talking about two things here: the gaze and interiorisation. … There is no need for arms, physical violence, material constraints. Just a gaze. An inspecting gaze, a gaze which each individual under its weight will end by interiorisation to the point that he is his own overseer, each individual thus exercising this surveillance over, and against, himself.

In addition, entering the academic writing arena after over thirty years writing in other fields, I have encountered something I have not felt before: suspicion. I have felt suspicious of others. Would they steal my ideas? Would they misrepresent me? Would they misuse my work? This being new to me, I know it is not an emotional default position of mine nor has it come up in other situations where I have shared my work with writers. I am, therefore, supposing that the academic environment has created this unhealthy, isolating system for writers where the crucial aspect of giving and receiving feedback is rife with anxieties and difficulties.

Sue in Case Study 2, puts it thus:

> If you're looking at what can stop you writing, particularly in an academic context, it's (a) your audience and (b) people who might also be there either willing you to do it or in either very tacit or implicit ways inhibiting you. I've seen good supervision but I've also experienced very, very bad supervision, when you think, what are you scared of? And again, they're under pressure,

from the academy and from other things. But none of that is ever explicitly stated, it feels, you know that's all implicit and has not to be exposed, because, again, that's about vulnerability isn't it?

See under "Writing Strategies" in this chapter for a more healthy approach to the critical review.

Our Writer Self[3]

Huston (1998) advises that not being able to identify oneself as a writer — what she calls the "imposter syndrome" — is a block to getting on and doing it. On the other hand, defining oneself as a writer may also be fraught and give rise to a mass of mixed feelings. Author Atwood (2003, p. 23) calls writing the "dark art" and suggests it comes encumbered:

> A lot of people do have a book in them. ... But this is not the same as "being a writer". Or, to put it in a more sinister way: everyone can dig a hole in a cemetery, but not everyone is a grave-digger. The latter takes a good deal more stamina and persistence. It is also, because of the nature of the activity, a deeply symbolic role. As a grave-digger, you are not just a person who excavates. You carry upon your shoulders the weight of other people's projections, of their fears and fantasies and anxieties and superstitions.

Accepting the mantle of "writer" is not, therefore, a straightforward process. It may, in itself, be blocking, if it is accompanied by too many expectations — our own, and those perceived in, or received from, others. Atwood goes on to conceptualise writers as "twins" with an everyday persona and an "other, more shadowy and altogether more equivocal personage who shares the same body, and who, when no-one is looking, takes it over and uses it to commit the actual writing". (P. 32.) If we do, indeed, experience our writerly ego as the "other", as "shadowy" or "equivocal", then allowing that part of us free rein to write might be anxiety-laden.

In some ways, whenever we write, we take on an "identity" as a writer. We may identify ourselves as a non-writer, a good writer, a bad writer, a struggling writer. These notions of us as a writer will be developed by past experiences and feedback. We may be less easy with the label of "academic writer" if there is something in our own background which somehow suggests that academia is not for us.

> [Students and academics] need to discuss the writer-reader relationship explicitly from the point of view of self-representation. All too often an understanding of "the reader" is limited to issues of background, knowledge, expectations and/or considerate use of signposting. The issue of what impression the reader is going to receive of the writer as a person remains covert, yet this may be exactly what is subconsciously bothering the writer. (Ivanič, 1998, p. 340.)

I am a writer first and then an academic. There are times when an uneasiness creeps in: will the readers of this book dismiss what I have to say because they will get the impression of me as not being academic enough? It is a risk I am willing to take, both in the style I am using and in making this admission because I believe I have something useful to offer those struggling with writing in the academic environment. On the other hand, what is a discomfort for me may be something much stronger and more arresting of the writing hand for another.

Taking on the notion of writer at all, or of academic writer in particular, may not be easy. Yet allowing at least a part of ourselves to "be a writer" is a significant step. It leads us to valuing what we are doing as something worthwhile and, consequently, we feel more able to give time and space to it, we are more able to resist, when necessary, the other calls on our energy and demands from others. Rather than declare "I am a writer", it might be easier to think of taking on the role of writer or finding that writerly fragment within us. There are ideas for encouraging this under the "Writing Strategies" section of Chapter 1.

Summary Box

The affective domain is often at the core of a writing block and so worth exploring. Feelings of shame (in all their complexities), fear of criticism and audience, and not being easy with the role of writer, can all underlie a halt in our writing.

WRITING STRATEGIES

The affective domain underpinning writing blocks is an important one to acknowledge and explore, preferably with an understanding peer, colleague or supervisor. Just knowing that feelings such as shame or the "imposter syndrome" are in the mix may be enough, allowing us to understand better why we have stopped writing and then move on.

Getting the support of those around you is crucial. In Chapter 5, I talk more about how and when feedback is important and how to cultivate a writing community for ourselves. However, to briefly address the issue of the "critical review" here, I offer the following guidance:

For those doing the critique or review:

– Be specific. Don't generalise about the whole piece, but give specific points where it can be improved.
– Be enabling. Give examples of how these improvements might be made or models of the kind of writing required.
– Be generous. Don't allow your own emotional baggage to get in the way of encouraging a fellow traveller.

For those receiving the critique or review:

– Think: this is about your work, not about you.
– Write down the salient points from the review. Then leave for at least a week before considering it, so that the initial sting can pass.

CHAPTER 2

- Work out what's non-negotiable for you (what you're not prepared to change at any price) and for the reviewer (what's essential to get your piece accepted, as opposed to what's merely desirable).
- Understand that there may be other factors at play here that have nothing to do with nurturing innovative thinking and writing. Reviewers have an affective domain as well.

It is also possible to get to know what emotional strands lie behind your writing blocks through writing exercises. I have grouped them here under the heading "Getting to Know Your Writing Blocks". Before going on, if you have not already done so, please look at the "Read This First!" section in the introduction to this book.

Getting to Know Your Writing Blocks

All writers have writing blocks. Examining them and working with them can give us clues as to where they stem from. Perhaps they come from past experiences of writing or feedback on our writing or from our own sense of ourselves as writers. Writer Godwin (2001, pp. 75–77) describes her own encounter with her writing block:

> What I did discover, however, when I sat down to write my first full-length non-fiction work, was that a new inner critic materialised out of the shadows with her own set of no-nos. She blew on my heart instincts with her dry-ice breath and often smothered my creative joy. I have an old working relationship with my fiction-writing inner critic, a picky, prissy, buttoned-up man with a smile that is both sinister and obsequious. (Once, when he was being exasperating, I drew his portrait.) His job consists mostly of wringing his hands and being fearful that I'll fail at being marvellous. I've learned to coexist with him over the years, but she was something new.
> She cast herself in the form of a beautiful icy woman in a sari, the ghost figure of a professor I had in graduate school, who once beseeched me in her elegant Oxbridge accent to write a "real" thesis not one of those "creative ones", ... In some ways I profited from her manifestation. When you are writing a work "based on facts and reality", you must be accountable. You must cite your sources. ... But on the negative side, she kept squelching me. ... "You may write in your own author's voice, since it's the only one you've got, but keep your personal experiences out of it."
> She prevailed to the extent that when I turned in what I thought was the finished manuscript, the editor respectfully sent back twelve single-spaced pages of suggestions, almost all of which had to do with putting more of myself into the book. (Pp. 75–77.)

What does your writing block sound like? Does its voice or form of words remind you of anyone? Does it have anything useful to tell you? Perhaps spending a short time on one of these exercises will give you a clearer picture? Below I suggest some writing exercises for getting to know more about your writing blocks. It's possible to do them on your own (though there is also a description of how one of them can be introduced to a group). Don't take too long on them and spend a short time noticing — not judging — what you have put and wondering how it might relate to your experiences. It can be fun to do these exercises with other people whom you trust. It is always useful to take your thoughts and insights gained to a supportive colleague, tutor or supervisor. The "getting to know your writing blocks" exercises comprise:

- Letters.
- The zoo/the nature reserve.
- A conversation.

Letters   To help her write her journal, Anne Frank imagined she was addressing a friend called "Kitty". What she did instinctively makes sense if we accept the relationality of writing. To write is to seek to speak to someone, even if it is initially ourselves. We are reaching out to initiate a conversation. Letters are, perhaps, a bit of an old-fashioned way to communicate; maybe I should be suggesting email or text or a social networking posting. Whatever works for you, as long as it is inviting of a response.

To begin with, have a go at contacting the writer-in-you. Try and make the first "letter" encouraging and include only a few key, specific questions. It may help if you give the writer-in-you a name, a name you've always liked, perhaps one you've always wished you'd been called, or maybe the name of a favourite author.

> Dear Hannah,
> You've done really well to get this far considering everything that has happened in the last few months. I know you're worried about getting everything done within the deadline, but I have confidence you'll get there.
>
> You seem particularly anxious today, what does that feel like? What's your biggest fear?
> Yours affectionately, KE

Now, I wonder how the writer-in-you might reply?

> Dear KE
>
> Well thanks for the interest, sometimes I don't think you realise how hard it is for me to keep going. Right now I feel like there's all these words swirling around at the base of my throat but I can't seem to get the right ones out in any kind of order that makes sense. And the word count is going up so slowly, I'm sure the computer isn't functioning right. Do you think it only counts hyphenated words as one?
>
> What's my biggest fear? Right now, making an utter fool of myself when people read this and sneer. Better not to finish, then. Well, that's an age-old one, isn't it? We both recognise that.
> Cheers, Hannah.

CHAPTER 2

> Aw Hannah, do we have to go round that particular loop again? If we don't finish, we'll never achieve what we've wanted to do since we were teenagers. That's a long time to be wanting to do something and not getting there. So let's not blow it this time. Sounds like you need some reassurance that what you're writing is worth reading. But you can also remember how much people have appreciated what they've read so far. Does that help?
> Yours affectionately, KE.
>
> Dunno, maybe, cheers, H.

I'm suggesting that the writer-in-you could be a starting point for this type of exercise; however you may be drawn to initiating an exchange between you and someone or something else. Here are a few other possibilities (please note, these letters are always unsent even if they are to real people):

- Your writing block, maybe with the question: What are you afraid of? Or: What are you defending me from? Or: What have you got to tell me?
- Your essay/article/thesis/book.
- Someone in the real world who you feel wants to stop you from writing.
- Someone in the real world who you feel wants to encourage you to write.

The zoo[4]   You are visiting a zoo or a safari park. Suddenly you see your writing block in one of the cages or enclosures. You are safe from it on the other side of the bars and you can take the time to study it. As quickly as you can, write down the responses to these questions:

- What does it look like?
- What does it smell like?
- What is the texture of its skin or outer coat?
- What noises is it making?
- What is it eating?
- What does it prefer to eat?
- Where does it sleep?
- Where does it hide?
- What is it afraid of?
- What is its prey?
- What preys on it?
- How does it reproduce?
- What makes it happy?
- Something you don't know about it.

From what you've now garnered from these questions, write an information card about your writing block, its habits and habitat. You may want to accompany the text with illustrations.

Writing Exercise, an Example: The Nature Reserve

This is an adaption of "the zoo" used by a senior lecturer in clinical psychology with her students. She planned to ask them to think of their clinical literature review/psychometric compendium and answer these questions:

– What type of animal is it?
– Describe it in detail
– How does it move?
– What does it feed off?
– Where does it live?
– Where does it hide?
– What is it scared of?
– Can you approach it?
– If so, how do you approach it?

She was then going to ask them to write an explanatory notice about it to go on a board at the nature reserve, the notices would then be shared in a small group. Finally the students would write a short reflection on what they had learnt/gained insight on as a result of the exercise.

She explains what happened: "Above was my plan for the nature reserve exercise. In the end we did it all except that the reflection at the end happened as a discussion rather than further writing. That felt more appropriate.

"I told the trainees that it was an exercise in using metaphor and explained that you could potentially use if for a clinical situation, placement situation, anything really but that as the clinical literature review was high on the horizon I thought we'd try it with that as the focus. I asked them to suspend disbelief or concerns about what I was asking them to do and just to go with it, to write down what came into their head without thinking too much about it. I explained that they wouldn't have to read out what they were writing. I read out each of the questions above in turn to them, allowing them time to write in between. I asked the next question when the majority of them had stopped writing. They responded well and all seemed to find they were able to write.

"After asking all the questions I explained that we were going to make a board with information about animals in a nature reserve and that I wanted them to write a short description of their animal as you would find in a zoo/reserve. I had taken in crayons so they could draw as well as write about their animals. We got coloured paper and they could choose how they presented their animal. Some just wrote a few words on a post-it note, others drew their animal and wrote, one used the writing to form part of their drawing. They enjoyed this part of the process and were pretty creative about it. They then stuck their pieces on a couple of flip-chart pieces of paper which we stuck together and they named 'the reserve'.

CHAPTER 2

> **Writing Exercise, an Example: The Nature Reserve**
>
> "We then looked at all the animals; each person read out their description. The majority of animals were scary, often predatory, and some attacked or ate trainees. One or two were benign, even sweet. One was a buzzy wasp-type thing which kept buzzing around, always present and annoying. We then had a discussion about their thoughts about the exercise. They varied; some found it really helpful to name the beast, others who had a benign animal found it concerning that maybe they should be more scared. Some said it made them think they just had to get on with doing the work, i.e. face the beast. My concern was that for the majority, a piece of academic writing which was designed to mirror what they might do anyway in clinical practice and be useful for them on placement was perceived as an aggressive predatory beast which they were scared of.
>
> "Feedback from the trainees suggested that it was helpful although not for all. One person found that it was helpful to get thoughts about the piece of work onto paper and make fun of them. They were able to tackle the piece of work more easily afterwards. I think overall it was probably useful and I would do it again but would be more prepared for the discussion afterwards and managing the mix of those who were anxious and those who weren't.".

A conversation You are in a strange neighbourhood and you are thirsty and hungry. You find an establishment where you can get something to eat and drink. What is it? A pub? A café? A restaurant? Describe it inside and out. Once inside, you find you are sitting close to a person who you realise is your writing block out with a close friend of theirs. Describe your writing block. What are they eating and drinking? You hear your writing block's name; what is it? Now you hear that your writing block is talking to their friend about how they are feeling, what they are most afraid of, what they want to achieve, what is their most secret secret. Listen and note down what they are saying. Then the friend asks how they can support your writing block, what the writing block needs to feel more relaxed. Again, note down the replies. If you feel strong enough, you may want to ask to join the table and address your writing block directly.

Wolton (2006, pp. 179–180) describes a similar exercise she facilitated in a workshop where a conversation was created with what she terms "the Critic". "The workshop participants devised questions for their Critics: 'What do you want? How could you be useful to me? How could we work together? What is your wisdom? What is your secret?' By this point we were developing a sense of enquiry, able to stand back from the battle and observe exactly how it was being fought. Many of us were surprised to discover that there were alternatives other than destroying the Critic or being destroyed by it." (Pp. 179–180.)

CONCLUSION — TAMING THE DRAGONS

> Many artists begin a piece of work, get well along in it, and then find as they near completion that the work seems mysteriously drained of merit. It's no longer worth the trouble. To therapists, this surge of sudden disinterest … is a routine coping device employed to deny pain and ward off vulnerability. (Cameron, 1993, p. 68.)

We write with others in mind, whether consciously or unconsciously; others crowd in on our words. Writing reveals us, it reveals what we are less comfortable with, as well as our talents. We fear and yet we crave communication and encounter with both our selves and other people. We have anxieties about how we might appear, about failure, about success. We have difficulties viewing ourselves as writers. All this can arouse feelings of paralysis, anger, disinterest, boredom and shame which will get in the way of putting the words down. Our writing blocks — our dragons — may be keeping us safe from this "exposure" to others and to distress. Their intent may be less malicious, more protective. They might not want us to take risks, though they may be too risk-averse for the present situation.

Knowing that there is an affective domain to writing blocks is a first step. Exploring it (perhaps using the writing exercises above), discussing it with supportive people, maybe seeking some professional advice from a counsellor or writing coach are all useful responses. In the end, by acknowledging our dragons in our swamp and getting to know something about them, we will discover that they are not as ferocious as they at first seem.

CHAPTER 2

NOTES

1. See Chapter 1 for more information on the "writing journal".
2. This section is an adaption and expansion of a part of Evans (2011A).
3. This section is an adaption and expansion of a part of Evans (2011A).
4. Most of the exercises will be familiar to facilitators of, and participants in, writing workshops. They are derivative of what could be termed "classic" writing exercises (Bolton, 1999; Bolton, Field & Thompson, 2006) and I would be hard pressed to specify where I first came across them. "The zoo", however, was something I was first introduced to at a workshop run by Larry Butler (www.lapidus.org.uk/groups/scotland.php) and Ted Bowman (www.bowmanted.com).

CHAPTER 3

A VIEWPOINT

The Craft of Gaining Perspective in Academic Writing

Our map has brought us to a viewpoint, however, it is still difficult to gain perspective. Hills which seemed close by are many leagues away. The tide, which a moment ago was over the horizon, is rushing in, quickening the sand. From here we can see how paths converge and diverge and run parallel: the paths we have already taken — though we did not realise at the time how they interlinked — as well as the paths we have yet to take. In places they look confusingly entangled, whereas elsewhere they are distinct and bright.

INTRODUCTION

In academic writing we adopt a particular perspective. The perspective is analytical, critical, scholarly. A certain amount of detachment is desirable so that we can look at a topic with some objectivity. We are able to look at it in detail as well as set it into its larger context. The academic perspective is a constructed one; we craft it. It is not necessarily the most obvious or the most natural one to take. There are skills to constructing this view which can facilitate our writing, meaning we are less likely to become blocked.

In this chapter I will explore how we construct this perspective and how our writing might become blocked along the way. I will suggest some strategies for dealing with those blocks and for maintaining perspective. I will consider:

– The concepts of "attachment", "distance" and the "in-between" in the practice of writing.
– Writing blocks in this realm, including those caused by "parallel process".
– Writing strategies for managing these writing blocks.

ATTACHMENT, DISTANCE AND THE IN-BETWEEN

Attachment

> I am filled with you.
> Skin, blood, bone, brain, and soul.
> (Rumi, trans. from Barks et al., 1995.)

We become attached to our material in two ways. Firstly, whether we wholly know it or acknowledge it or not, we are drawn to a topic which has some kind of personal

CHAPTER 3

resonance. Indeed, this has significant advantageous effects. As Rudeston & Newton (2001, p. 209) state:

> If you have any choice at all about topics for your writing, one of the most important things you can do to facilitate your writing is to choose one that you care about and are interested in. Although some advisers warn against choosing topics with high personal relevance on the grounds that your appropriate objectivity will be impaired, this danger is small compared to the problems that arise when you try to write about something entirely divorced from your personal experience, concern or interest.

Having a connection, a fascination even, with an issue will make it easier for us to spend time with it and dig into it. We are more likely to bring forth something which is authentically our own, and, thereby, offer a different slant from that which has been written about many times before.

Secondly, within the post-modern, social-constructionist context of today's academia, there is a growing acceptance that the researcher is intertwined in some way with the researched. The notion that the observed is affected by being observed has credence within quantitative circles. Qualitative researchers Finlay and Evans (2009, p. 21) promulgate that the researcher is "implicated in the research process." They go on to develop the idea of a "co-creation" which involves researcher and participant, where the researcher is both witness to, as well as co-author of, the results. That there is an association, a bonding, between researcher and research subject is recognised in most fields; however, the weight and importance given to this varies depending on approach, method and underpinning philosophy. This cord tying the researcher together with the research may be perceived as substantial or as more of an insignificant strand. It might be acknowledged and reflected upon or it could be discounted and ignored. However, it does exist.

We can also attach to the activity of writing. Writing is a "flow" activity (Csikszentmihalyi, 1996); it can be totally absorbing. When it is, we will lose track of time, we will become fascinated by the words and how we can play with them, create with them. They become "mudpies" for our delight (Le Guinn, 2004, p. 60). Writing may also have "transitional significance" (Cashdan, 1988, p. 43). For a child, a "transitional object" is usually a toy or a favoured thing which brings security and comfort especially when the care giver is absent. The toy becomes a temporary or transient substitute for the care giver. It is also "transitional" in that it gives the child enough reassurance to be able to venture away from the care giver; it marks a transition into greater independence. In adulthood, things — or activities such as writing — may take on a "transitional significance", offering a sense of safety, of relief, of ease, of confidence, and, therefore, gaining in importance because of that.

We have notions of attachment, then, of being connected, linked to our research and our writing. In the therapeutic world the word "attachment" immediately takes us to the work of Bowlby (1988), Stern (1985), Wallin (2007), Gerhardt (2004) and many others who argue that early relationships can mould how we "attach" or connect to the world around us as we mature. I could not hope to do justice to all that has been written and observed about the way people do or do not bond within their lives and at the different points in their lives. For my purposes here, I just want to take the idea that some people choose to be, or have a tendency towards, distrusting close attachments; while others find it difficult to function without the presence of another person. The former might be conceptualised as someone who is constantly moving on from place to place, person to person, thing to thing; while the latter becomes almost like a shadow, finding it difficult to assert their difference or individuality. In general, I would suggest, the majority of us move along a continuum which links these two extremes, having tendencies to one or the other but also responding to environment and the people we are with.

The important detail here is that this is not only about "attachment" to people. We have an "attachment" inclination towards what we do as well, which includes our "attachment" to our topic and to our writing. Are we avoiding writing because that's a trait we have elsewhere in our lives? Are we feeling overwhelmed by our writing because becoming subsumed is something that is familiar to us? Is there something about the subject matter which might trigger either of these propensities. If we are writing about violence, for instance, and in our lives we would normally avoid conflictual people?

Summary Box

We "attach" to our topic and to our writing. This "attachment" will vary given the circumstance and our own personal inclinations. How would you say your are attaching to your present topic, for instance? Are you feeling submerged in it or are you avoiding it? Are these familiar feelings? Are they getting in the way of your writing? Notice and acknowledge how closely tied you feel to your present academic task.

Distance

Once we are connected to something, we are interacting with it. Even if we choose to avoid the connection, our interaction is in the turning of our back, in the walking away or round.

> All human interactions can be characterized by the degree of distance therein. Distancing is a means of separating oneself from the other, bringing oneself closer to the other, and generally maintaining a balance between the two states of separation and closeness. ... In actuality, distancing is a confluence of physical, emotional and intellectual elements. (Landy, 1996, p. 13)

As with relating to people, we can interact more effectively with a topic and our writing when we can gauge and regulate our distance from them. To do this, all aspects of ourselves — the physical, the emotional, the cognitive — are called into

CHAPTER 3

action; they have to work together. With the emphasis in academic writing being on the intellectual, this may lead us to ignore what is going on at the feeling or the physical levels which can block us.

Drawing from Landy again, an "overdistancing" leads to the divorced, uninterested position counselled against by Rudeston and Newton above, whereas an "underdistancing" leads to feeling overwhelmed and besieged. Both "overdistancing" and "underdistancing" can stop us from writing.

> **Case Study 1**
>
> If I get too immersed in a subject and suddenly I don't know who I am in that any more, then I leave it well alone. Because of the subject matter, it might push all my buttons, then I'm like floating off, just losing it, losing my sense of myself. … And I have to leave it, find myself again and then go round the other business, things I have to do, until I've got enough courage to go back into whatever it was that I lost me in, try again.

However, to get to grips with our material, we need both a sense of separation and a sense of closeness, without over- or under-distancing ourselves. At times our stance will be microscopic, intimate; at times it will be pulled back, looking at the bigger or more generalised scene. Todres (2007, p. 58) describes it thus: "In exercising 'closeness' I attempted to enter my informants' experiences and bring the 'heart' of these textures to language. In exercising 'distance' I entered a more academic moment and attempted to tease out some of the meanings in a more thematic way."

I do not wish to suggest a hierarchy here. It is not that distance is better than closeness or vice versa: both are needed within academic writing. What is required is what Landy (1996, p. 17) calls an "aesthetic distance" where "the individual plays both roles of participant and observer simultaneously; or he is able to move fluidly from one role to another, as appropriate."

Sometimes this requires something as simple as taking a break, walking away when we are beginning to feel subsumed by our material ("underdistanced"). Or perhaps, if we are beginning to feel disinterested or bored ("overdistanced"), making an effort to connect with the detail we find the most intriguing will keep us going.

> **Summary Box**
>
> "Teach us to care and not to care." (T.S. Eliot, 1954, p. 84.)
>
> Blocks to writing can come from being either overdistanced or underdistanced from our material. What we can aim for is Landy's "aesthetic distance" and to moving fluidly from closeness to distance and back. This fluidity of movement means we are less likely to get stuck in our writing.

The In-between

Writing is an act of mediation between our inner and outer realities. We write using information from inside us — our thoughts and/or our emotions and/or our physical feelings — and also information from the environment around us. For example, I might write about a tree which is outside my office window, describing what I see; however, at the same time I will be using knowledge and responses from inside me such as what I know about trees and what I feel about them. I am interested in trees, I enjoy them; the way I write about them will reflect that. If I was disinterested or afraid of them my description would come out in a different way.

Writing is part of what Winnicott terms the "perpetual human task of keeping inner and outer reality separate yet interrelated". And it calls upon an "intermediate area" for its resolution (1971, p. 3). This is what I call the "in-between". When we write fluently we are writing from this in-between, where our self and what is beyond our skin make contact. There is something on the outside which is finding a resonance with what is going on inside us, or vice versa. There is a correlation being made. I visualise this connection happening in an "in-between" place which Winnicott (1971, p. 15) likens to the "play area of the small child who is 'lost' in play". This is the kind of "play" which I talk about in Chapter 6; it is creative, it leads to open thinking, exploration and reflection.

This in-between is also about distance: it is a holding of the outside against the inside without allowing the two to collapse into one another. We are able to hold on to what is going on for us internally alongside our experience of us responding to the external world. Without it, we could either become over absorbed in our own thoughts and feelings, lost in them, overwhelmed with them. Or, on the other hand, we become too concerned with the external environment and lose our individual perspective. If I go back to my tree, without the in-between I would either slip into ruminations about my own emotional state or, alternatively, I would give a dry description reliant on how other people perceive trees, losing my own unique angle. Without the in-between we become less clear about what is stemming from our own response and what it is that we are observing. In the academic world, of course, this loss of clarity is particularly catastrophic as it is our capacity to say what is "subjective" and "objective" which at least partly defines a scholarly activity. Writing from this in-between, this "intermediate area of *experiencing*, to which inner reality and external life both contribute" (Winnicott, 1971, p. 3), is an essential, then, for academic endeavour.

> **Summary Box**
>
> Writing from the "in-between", the place where our internal reality meets the external reality, allows for open thinking, exploration and reflection. We do this by attending to, listening to, what is going on within us, while also connecting with what is going on around us. The in-between, maintained through gauging "distance" in our writing, assists in the clarification of what can be defined as "subjective" as opposed to "objective". Greater exploration, reflection and clarity help us to write more fluently.

CHAPTER 3

BLOCKS TO WRITING

Our attachment tendencies in our lives may suggest an inclination to detach from, or become over-immersed in, our work, which could bring our writing to a halt. However, it is possible to develop a more healthy attachment to our writing, one where the writing itself is a trustworthy friend, dependable, listening, accepting. The act of writing becomes a "defence against anxiety" (Winnicott, 1971), a touchstone, a "secure base" (Bowlby, 1988) from which to explore our world. The trick is — and it is a "trick" or a knack which can be enhanced through writing exercises such as the ones described below — to gauge and regulate distance from our writing and to encourage writing from the "in-between". And once we have this sense of surety in our writing, it is easier then to allow it to toddle off and be greeted — even criticised — by others, much as when children gain their independence from their parents.

Wallin (2007, p. 4) also suggests that a "secure attachment" can lead to a more reflective and mindful stance which acknowledges the "'*merely* representational nature' of our own beliefs and feelings". In other words, our truth is one of many perspectives and it can co-exist with others. We can then let the ideas, beliefs, viewpoints, including criticism, from others flow around us, taking on board what we need and leaving the rest where it is. If our writing has a "*merely* representational nature", then so do the opinions and thoughts of those around us, and the critical feedback we will inevitably receive won't stop us in our tracks. Instead we will be able to pick through it and extract what is useful for us in taking our writing forwards.

"Parallel Process"

As has already been discussed, our subject matter will almost inevitably have some personal resonance for us. There are indications from neuroscience that the mirror neurones which are triggered in response to another's emotional state (Stern, 2004) to create empathy[1] can also be activated through reading (Evans, 2009; Carr, 2011). As writers we are also our first readers. This act of reading, then, can create a further sense of this text having an emotional significance for us. If the material we are writing about and, therefore, reading is affecting, perhaps disturbing, then we may want to pull away from it. This can block our writing.

Furthermore, there's the potential for what could be termed a "parallel process". I am taking the term parallel process from the psychotherapeutic world, where something that is happening in the relationship between client and therapist is "paralleled" or mirrored in the relationship between the therapist and the person supervising them. So, for instance, if the therapist finds themselves uncharacteristically angry with their supervisor, by acknowledging this and exploring this, the therapist might find out some useful information about the dynamic between them and their client. The key word here is "uncharacteristic"; the emotion in the supervisor/supervisee interaction should feel unfamiliar or aberrant. Others before me have taken parallel process out of this narrow context, for instance, Davies (1997). I am now going to consider how it can illuminate a writing block within the academic environment.

It first came strongly to my attention when I was writing an academic article based on a phenomenologically inspired case study of an individual's writing journey (Evans, 2011). I was finding my writing slowed by the unusually heightened anxiety I was feeling, especially around the peer review process. I identified this with my interviewee's anxieties around meeting others' expectations. Realising this both helped me to get on with my own writing, and, in addition, brought me closer to the experience I was trying to shed light on: that of my interviewee.

I began to talk about this to colleagues and explore some of the literature, and other examples came to the surface. An academic in the field of psychology was struggling to complete a paper for a journal. She wrote: "Anyway, at this stage I think the whole thing is deeply flawed and I am plagued with doubt and negative thoughts about the paper, the enterprise (to challenge existing models of understanding — how grandiose!) and being unworthy to do it: what gives me the right? Who do I think I am...?" (Personal communication.) Overall she was battling to continue with the article because she felt that she would not be understood, that her thoughts on the subject would be discounted; indeed, that she would be treated much as those in her study had been by medical professionals.

Another example came from Marie[2], a clinical psychologist who had just completed her doctorate research:

> **"Parallel Process" as a Writing Block — an Example**
>
> I was researching in the field of diabetes management for children. I was interested in how the beliefs about diabetes and varying emotional distress levels between parent and child would impact on the management of the illness. I had to recruit 60 dyads, from three clinics across hospital sites in three cities. This was done one day a week. I had questionnaire packs with measures for anxiety, beliefs and management of diabetes.
>
> In the middle of all this I had to change supervisor. I wanted my new supervisor to understand and guide me and she needed to learn herself and also to let me go through the process of managing the diabetes that I didn't want.[3] We never knew if we were getting it right. About this time, I also realised that I had a huge dislike of maths and all the statistics began to seem really complicated and overwhelming and in analysing the results I didn't understand why I was doing the analyses. I knew I had to keep going with it, that it would all fail if I didn't, but it made no sense. By this point I couldn't get my mind to hold it all in place and I wished I could just get rid of it or someone would do it for me.
>
> My supervisor was very aware of this. Feeling stuck, being overwhelmed in the detail, wanting an exact answer, worrying whether I was managing the project well enough. She asked if I usually approached my work this way. On

CHAPTER 3

> **"Parallel Process" as a Writing Block — an Example (Continued)**
>
> reflection I said I did not. We wondered what was going on then. My supervisor had noticed that she felt pressured to tell me exactly what to do and that wouldn't help me learn and that there wasn't a definite answer to things but space for interpretation. I thought it was just all too serious to be left to the realms of interpretation. I was tired and sick of it and it took over my life, which I wanted back. I explained that I felt like I needed to kick and scream and sit on the floor with my arms crossed, saying, "I'm not doing it and no-one can make me. You sort it out." Whilst my supervisor said, "I'm new to this too."
>
> She raised the idea of a parallel process occurring between the research and supervision. It felt good to become reflective again. By this point in the write-up I felt so scientific and restricted in the use of language and thought, I was practically craving process and adjectives. Something wholesome and nourishing rather than the stupid, reductionist diet I was forced to be on.
>
> For me, naming it was the hugest relief. It was still difficult to write it out in a scientific style, I had to write it normally and translate it to the correct style but the reflection on the parallel process had broken it down into steps and so it felt more manageable. It was still difficult to hold in mind as it felt so endless, diagrams helped.
>
> The biggest relief was that all the emotional turmoil and conflict was lifted. That made thinking easier and the analysis more manageable. It also changed how I felt in the supervision relationship and rather than conflict, it felt like we were back in it together. We could talk and share it more collaboratively and think about what the experience had meant, what the families were saying and what we knew about diabetes to create an understanding of the results. Before that it had felt like a problem in us; naming it separated it. (Personal communication.)

Marie and her supervisor had become caught up in a parallel process which mirrored in many ways the experience of some children and parents trying to manage diabetes. Marie felt that she didn't want this research (this disease); it was becoming overwhelming, unmanageable; she wanted somebody else to "sort it out". She felt like acting in quite a childlike way, sitting on the floor and kicking and screaming. Her supervisor was also new to the research (disease) and was having to learn as she went along. She felt as if she had to step in and give immediate answers. In this case, naming the parallel process and becoming reflective helped move the writing on. Marie explains what other strategies assisted: "Mapping out the results visually. Breaking down the problem. My supervisor explaining why she was correcting something, rather than just doing it. These strategies are very similar to what was recommended to diabetes clinics to improve management of the illness for young people." (Personal communication.)

Consultant clinical health psychologist and doctoral and PhD supervisor Dr Dorothy Frizelle, who I interviewed for this book, suggests that parallel process is "systematically present to a lesser or greater degree [in research] depending on the subject matter and how immersed that person is with the clinical subject matter and the patients and with their write-up. I'm not saying that with the people where it is less apparent, they are less immersed, but with some people it does seem to be more apparent."

She gave an example from her work with students. Adam was working on a dissertation looking at the help seeking behaviour of cardiac patients with erectile dysfunction. He was asking, what stops them from seeking medical assistance. Dr Frizelle describes what had happened:

> He was really resistant to seeking my help. It only became apparent because we reached a point in our supervisor-trainee relationship when I was really cross with him and sent him a stinky email saying I am unable to supervise you if you do not send me things, and copied it to the head of department of the time. It was only at that point that he came in and it was a really emotional session because he was admitting to not feeling potent enough, not feeling good enough. And we were able to talk about that. And my part in the parallel process was as the female doctor that the male patient wouldn't go to because they wouldn't want the female doctor to make judgements about their virility. Generally I would have been able to stand back, but I had not realised I was in the process because it was so particularly powerful. I was making judgements and being quite harsh. He realised he was mirroring participants' passivity to help-seeking. And I had been uncharacteristically poor or slow in responding to him. I had taken on the role of ensuring that he would finish rather than sitting with him and saying, "Well, what is going on with your draft?" And that's a parallel with the doctor saying, "I'm sorry you have to take your medication or you could die of your heart problem, I don't want to know about erectile dysfunction. Sorry, but the priority is the cardiac treatment."

The parallel process for both Adam and Marie had made it hard to write. However, Dr Frizelle suggests that it can also be a tool. "It's really useful as a tool for giving the student/supervisor information, helping us make sense. It helps us to have insight into data: whether it's verbal data from interviews, or numbers data, it can help us make sense of relationships or differences. This is reflected in the writing. You can really tell the people who know these patients and have an understanding and have been engaged, and the people who have written it as a writing exercise, as an academic exercise. I think that shows to me as external examiner as well. It's so apparent in the quality of discussion sections of the papers."

CHAPTER 3

> **Summary Box**
>
> Writing blocks can occur if we find ourselves too overwhelmed or too distanced from our material or our writing. Finding the fluidity to move from intimacy to distance helps us to keep writing, as well as assisting in the scholarly need for a clear distinction between "subjectivity" and "objectivity". Becoming securely "attached" to our writing brings a greater trust in our writing ability and, therefore, a greater openness to the usefulness of critical feedback. A "parallel process" between research material and how we write has the potential to block us as well as the potential to give us new information.

WRITING STRATEGIES

How can we regulate distance in our writing? What is it that allows us to gain perspective of the larger context when we feel overwhelmed, or re-engage when we feel detached from what we are writing? What happens if we feel caught up in a "parallel process" which is halting us? Marie suggested that acknowledgement of the issues, good supervision and visual representations all assisted her. Mind maps, for instance, are diagrammatic tools which could be helpful. They group words or ideas on the page and then show how they might be linked. When working with mind maps, it's best to write the words or statements down as quickly as possible, rather like the "free writing" introduced in Chapter 1.

This is an example of a mind map:

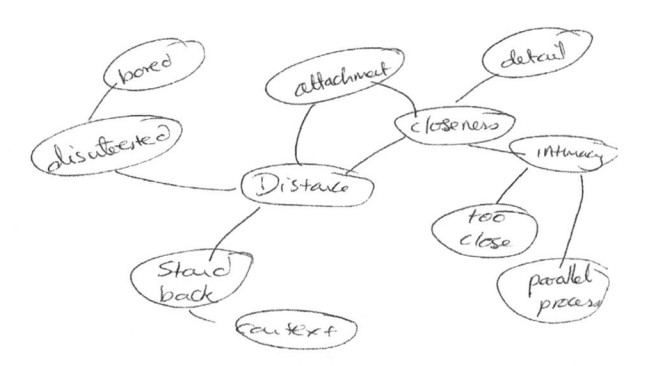

[Mind map diagram with nodes: bored, disinterested, attachment, closeness, detail, intimacy, Distance, too close, Stand back, context, parallel process]

Another approach would be to experiment with gauging and regulating distance using the creative writing technique of shifting "person" or "point of view".

As noted in Chapter 5, different disciplines have different conventions when it comes to the presence or absence of the author. Generally speaking, the more scientific and quantitative the field, the more the "I" of the writer will be missing and the more the passive third-person writing will be favoured. The more qualitative the work, the more the "I" of the author will be present, acknowledged and reflected upon. This is how a piece of writing will be required to end up. When beginning to write about our research material, however, experimenting with the position of the author can help us to tread the line between feeling too overwhelmed by our material and feeling so disconnected that we lose interest.

Shifting "person" or "point of view" is a simple grammatical exercise, but the effects can be significant. When we write we choose to write in a particular "person", ie "I walk" is the "first person". We can choose to write in the "third person", ie "she walks" or "he walks". Or in the "second person", ie "you walk". Before reading on, please have a look at the "Read this First!" section in the introduction to this book.

Exercises in Shifting "Person" Or "Point of View": Getting Going

Find some pieces written in the "first person" and the "third person" in magazines, newspapers, on the internet or in books. Notice whether there are any different effects on you as the reader, especially in terms of "distance". How close do you feel to the action in each case? How close do you feel to the people in the piece? Then try the "Taking a walk" exercise described in Chapter 1. Write it initially using the first person, then try out the third or the second person by simply changing "I" to "she" or "he" or "you". Again, notice whether this makes a difference to you as both writer and reader in terms of how distant you feel from the action.

Experiences will vary, of course, however, you may notice feeling closer to what's being described when the "first person" is being used. The "third person" stance often gives more a sense of being an observer, of watching something unfold, rather than being part of it. In my experience as a writer, using "you" can be very interesting; sometimes it feels intimate and warm, at other times it can feel accusatory and harsh, depending on the content.

To increase your flexibility in terms of shifting point of view in writing, you could use your writing journal (see Chapter 1, under "Writing Strategies"). Write a week's worth of entries using the first person, then a week's worth using the third person and finally a week's worth using the second person. The entries would still be about what you are doing, you would just be writing it in a different "person". For example:

> In one of my recent journal entries I wrote, "It's OK for me to walk away as long as I walk back again, which is what I'm trying to do today. Suddenly deciding I need to sort the bookshelves is a sure sign of procrastination, of avoiding. What am I avoiding? Fear and anxiety. Yet anxiety comes from not doing."
> Written in the third person it becomes, "It's OK for her to walk away as long as she walks back again, which is what she's trying to do today. Suddenly deciding

CHAPTER 3

> she needs to sort the bookshelves is a sure sign of procrastination, of avoiding. What is she avoiding? Fear and anxiety. Yet anxiety comes from not doing."
> And in the second person, "It's OK for you to walk away as long as you walk back again, which is what you're trying to do today. Suddenly deciding you need to sort the bookshelves is a sure sign of procrastination, of avoiding. What are you avoiding? Fear and anxiety. Yet anxiety comes from not doing."

Shifting "person" is a question of grammar, and yet the effect it has on meaning and on the writer and reader goes far beyond this. It is a useful technique which can help us to regulate distance in our writing, both for ourselves and for those we are communicating with.

Exercises in Shifting "Person" or "Point of View": Our Academic Work

We don't always have to stay as "I" the academic. Perhaps we could write as the phenomenon we are exploring? What does the mould we are looking down our microscope at have to say? What does the unanswered questionnaire have to say? What does the unwritten essay have to tell us?

Moving from your position of observer to take the position of the observed can give a different perspective on what you are writing about and, therefore, make it easier to keep going with it. In some ways it is a simple grammatical shift as described in the section above, from "she", "he" or "it" to "I"; however, the resulting understanding can be far more significant.

For example, in this chapter I use the theoretical concept of "parallel process". I rely heavily on Davies's (1977, p. 114) definition of parallel process. She says, "Parallel process may be seen as the playing-out of experiences that are unresolved and out of awareness. Our past experiences cause us to recreate habitual patterns of behaviour in our interaction with others that parallel the original." The parallel process is an "it" to be observed. What would happen if I became the parallel process?

> I am parallel process, I am a wheel within a wheel, a cog within a mechanism, a mirror. I spin out the relationships between people, create the cloth of how they interact, with a pattern which is recognisable, traditional, familiar, though not necessarily kind. My threads intertwine and twist. They may pull tight and snag and look ugly. They may slide between each other, comfortably, beautifully. They mirror a more ancient fabric, one which has been played out before and yet never looked at properly. If my weave were to be studied, would a different choice be made? Would the hues be slightly altered, the zigzag tempered? I do not make these choices; I merely function, I am the machinery.

Parallel process as an idea was introduced to me during my training as a counsellor and I have had cause to discuss it in both written work and in the supervision of my client work. So it is a notion that I have found beneficial to help explicate what is happening in certain relationships. I started considering that it might act as a writing block and then discovered people who had experienced it as such. This is the first time I have turned the "it" into an "I", though the writing is obviously informed by the number of times I have cast myself as observer of the parallel process. I think this first-person piece does give a slightly different perspective; in particular the view that it is an apparatus which threads between all relationships and it can also be "beautiful".

I wrote this before I interviewed Dr Frizelle. She echoed this idea that it could be "beautiful" in that it gives new information; also in that it can facilitate writing when the relationship being paralleled is a positive and nurturing one.

Summary Box

Moving perspective by grammatically changing the "person" is a writing skill which can be acquired. Once we are relatively adept at it, we can use it to gauge and manage the distance we have from our material, moving in when we need to and taking on the observer perspective when appropriate. This means that, rather than become disinterested or overwhelmed, we are able to keep writing. Moving our perspective provides us with new information which also keeps our words flowing.

CONCLUSION

When writing academically we aspire towards a scholarly perspective. Conventions around this will vary depending on the discipline, especially in the use of "I" and the ostensible presence or absence of the author. However, a scholarly perspective will want some use of detail ("closeness") and some review of context ("distance"), as well as clarity around the "subjective" and "objective" stances that we may purport to employ. This is a constructed perspective. We can develop our capacity for constructing it through the use of "distance". However, being "overdistanced" or "underdistanced" from our material or becoming caught up in a "parallel process" can hinder this construction of the scholarly perspective and can stop us from writing.

All the strategies below can assist us to develop the skills for the scholarly perspective and to become more fluent in our writing:

– Being aware of how we "attach" or not to our material and writing.
– Working towards an "aesthetic distance" and fluidity when it comes to writing in terms of "distance" from our material.
– Cultivating the "in-between" writing space.
– Recognising the pitfalls and potential of "parallel process".
– Using visual representations such as mind maps.
– Becoming more adept at the possibilities raised by exploring the grammatical use of the different "person" in writing.

CHAPTER 3

Getting a different perspective

NOTES

1. Empathy is "the capacity to think and feel oneself into the inner life of another person". (Kohut, 1984, quoted in DeYoung, 2003, p. 50.)
2. A pseudonym.
3. I had asked for a narrative written quite freely and Marie had purposely not rechecked it before sending it to me. When I pointed out the missing word "research" in this sentence, she said it had not been a deliberate omission. It perhaps shows the closeness of the parallel process even though this was written some time after the experience.

CHAPTER 4

FINDING THE STORY

The InterPlay Between Narrative and Writing Blocks

Our path inevitably leads us to a thicket, a briar grown tangled and sharp and woody over many thousands of years. All that is within is asleep waiting for us to bring it to wakefulness. There is one gate still accessible amongst all the thorns and beyond it is a way through to the feast, somnolent yet full of promise. The gate is too high and has no decent footholds; we cannot climb it. Its key lies in one of the three boxes at our feet. They have to be opened in the correct sequence for the key to be relinquished and we only have three chances to get it right. It is a conundrum, it is a riddle, which will take all our mental agility to solve.

INTRODUCTION

We are all storytellers. In order to figure out our experience of our world and to communicate it to others, we set events and ideas into a sequence: "This happened and then that." We look for causation, for what occurred because of something else. We make linkages; for instance, that extra pint the night before meant we botched our maths exam, so we went to a different university from the one we intended, took modules we'd not even considered before, which led us into a particular field of research and so on. Describing what took place, finding a pattern or order, suggesting or demonstrating causation, explaining apparent randomness: all these are storytelling skills. We have them and we use them every day. Narrative — telling stories — is fundamental to the way humans understand and create meaning and knowledge both about themselves and the world around them. It is "the primary form by which human experience is made meaningful…" It "functions to organise elements of awareness into meaningful episodes". (Polkinghorne, 1988, p. 1.)

Academic writing is also a story, a way of organising elements into a meaningful progression which can be communicated to others. We are able to use the storytelling capacity we employ daily to begin to construct our academic narrative. Unfortunately, we may not realise this; we may think that academic writing is somehow different (and indeed it does have its own conventions, see Chapter 5). Yet, despite it having its own rules, academic writing does still use the basic storytelling techniques we are already familiar with. And we may become blocked if we stifle our natural tendency to seek the story.

CHAPTER 4

In addition, narrative is also a way to make or find meaning. By not using our storytelling capabilities, we may become stymied because we are shutting ourselves off from a way through to understanding. It is in ordering the events or ideas in some kind of arrangement that we can begin to comprehend how one thing works with or against another.

And there is one further element to our story of narrative and writing blocks: we have our own story of ourselves as a writer. For example, I consider myself a writer now, yet within my story of myself becoming that writer are: the remedial reading lessons I had at school; the initial failure to get published and work as a journalist; the experience I have of working therapeutically with creative writing. These are events I have collected (I dare say there are others I have discounted) to which I have given importance within my story of how I became the writer I am today. The elements we choose for our own story of our selves as writer will affect how we see our writerly self now, whether we view it as capable or not, as reliable or not, as comfortable or not. By looking at this story we have, and, perhaps, reassembling it or discovering new elements to it, we can construct a different narrative which could help us to be more at ease with the part of us who writes and find that we are able to write with greater facility. Chapter 2 and Case Study 3 explore the idea that a sense of being an "imposter" as an academic writer can be a block to writing. The story we tell of ourselves as writer will play a large part in how crushing the weight of the "imposter" syndrome might be. Reshaping our story can potentially mean we feel less of an "imposter" and can take on the writer mantle with greater alacrity.

In this chapter I will expand on:

- Academic writing as narrative.
- Narrative as a technique for finding meaning.
- The narrative of ourselves as writers.
- Writing blocks connected with these ideas about narrative.
- Writing strategies for addressing these writing blocks.

ACADEMIC WRITING AS NARRATIVE

I ask students, "What's the story you're trying to tell?" Students who read — and it doesn't matter what they read; it could be novels — write better because they absorb style and they absorb story telling. (Senior lecturer in biochemistry, personal communication.)

In forming an explanation or presenting an issue to another we will automatically find the story. We will sequence what we want to say in a way which pinpoints a beginning and then links notions or happenings together until we reach some kind of ending. The beginning may not really be the beginning: how can we be certain when we first engaged with a particular question, and what about others who have touched on it before? The ending may not be particularly conclusive and, in any case, it is unlikely that this will be the last time this topic is taken up. The links we find, the events we choose to highlight, are the ones which appear seminal at that time. Someone else could make a different selection, as might we at a different time or place. There is little that is inevitable about this narrative, yet it helps us to transmit our account onto someone else.

As humans we are drawn to narrative at a deeply primal level. When we say, "That makes sense," what we most often mean is, "I've got the story." While exploring our subject matter we collect many, many bits of information from a myriad of sources, we sense that they are key to what we are trying to say, and yet they don't seem to fit together. This can leave us feeling overwhelmed, unable to find a route in, a place to start. There seem to be so many threads to pull at that we cannot tease out the one to form the beginning of our tale. We may start lots of outlines or mind maps, fill up pages with notes, and yet the piece we want to write eludes us. The words on the page may be mounting up, yet they remain messy, disparate, unshaped.

For example, with this chapter, I had written down its heading very early on in my thinking about this book. I had notes and references about the importance of narrative to the construction of meaning and self. I knew that this was somehow linked to some writing blocks, and yet I had started on this chapter numerous times and had ended up with seemingly unrelated snatches of text and some quotations, scattered like self-contained planets in a solar system. But planets are not self-contained, they work upon each other through gravity; and somehow I could take a spaceship through this galaxy and show how the forces of narrative and writing blocks coexist and exert influence, the one on the other. Could I make this journey and show the invisible lines which tie the two together and take my fellow voyagers along with me? I felt re-energised. I did have a story to tell.

I enjoy fairy tales. Not the sanitised versions which we started to imbibe in recent centuries, but the ones which our oral telling ancestors used to entertain, to inform and to look at the unexplained, the curious, the shadows at the edges of their existence. Each storyteller would re-fabric the basic story for their own purposes and the tales would be passed on, altered at each retelling according to the needs of the fabricator and the listener. Fairy tales hold within them the key elements and structures of all stories (for more, see under "Writing Strategies"); they are tools for construction. Knowing this, when I tried again to break the deadlock on this chapter, I began with: "Once upon a time a writer sat down to write. She wanted to write, or at least, she knew vaguely what she wanted to write. Still she hung back. 'I'll write just for an hour,' she told herself. 'And I won't worry too much what I put down; I won't try to get it perfect or even nearly right. I'll just see what comes.' Such reassurances didn't help. 'Maybe it's just that I have got nothing to say. I mean not in general, but on this topic. I know it was what came to mind really quickly, but it's losing its gloss, it doesn't seem that crucial anymore…'" And on for a paragraph, until I put down, "And yet, and yet, there are words sort of lingering about in the ether, if only she could net them and put them into some kind of order." The word "ether" set me thinking about each aspect I had identified being a satellite, exerting influence on the other, and it gave me a possible way into the story I was trying to tell. I knew my "Once upon a time…" beginning would not make it into the final cut, but it was enough to get me rolling.

However, isn't storytelling associated with fiction, with the imagination, with making something up? The idea that it could be linked to academic writing is already a stumbling block. Academic writing involves something far more complex, more serious, than storytelling, isn't that so? The idea that academic writing is different from, even opposed to, our more natural tendency to tell stories means that we may get stuck because we don't know how to approach it. We are pulled towards narrative creation, and yet we have the sense that we have to put aside all the skills we have in this area and find others. Knowing that academic writing is indeed about narrative, about storytelling, means we can stop searching for another method which might appear more scholarly, and we can just go with our innate instincts, as, at the very least, a way into our material.

For instance, Case Study 3 interviewee, Sarah, was struggling with knowing where to start, having done a literature review and collected a mountain of research notes and ideas. She wrote to me, "At one point [my supervisor] suggested trying to give the dreaded paper more of a narrative to try and get to grips with it. I then tried a very creative approach to it — writing vignettes about three different women (of different time periods) and their experience of pregnancy as influenced by the available technology. It really felt much more like creative writing and I ended up with three 'short stories' about these women. The idea was then to turn these into a paper about the effect of technology (scans in particular) on women's experience of pregnancy, maybe even using extracts from the vignettes in the final paper. However, I didn't do anything else with it. ... I'm now thinking of going back to this. I found it really useful, as it made the whole issue more 'real'." (Personal communication.)

> **Summary Box**
>
> As humans we tell stories every day. We have the skills to describe events, link them and show causality or explain randomness. We can use these narrative skills in our academic writing.

NARRATIVE AS A TECHNIQUE FOR FINDING MEANING

Telling stories, creating a narrative, is one way that humans have of finding meaning, both in terms of daily life and of more existential and cosmic questions. Roland Barthes (in Polkinghorne, 1988) said that there has never existed a people who have not fashioned narratives. People — individuals and cultures — require a narrative to make sense of themselves and the world around them and then to communicate this to others, in order to fix and strengthen that understanding (Woods, 1999; Bold, 2012; Martin, 2000; Polkinghorne, 1988).

> Narrative plays a crucial role in almost every human activity. Narrative dominates human discourse, and is foundational to the cultural processes that organize and structure human behaviour and experience. Narrative is also fundamental to human reality and our understanding of human experience. It offers important ways to encode human truth and experience, and, in turn, share knowledge and insights with others. It therefore is important to realize that narrative is not simply a literary form, but is a basic property of the human mind. (Hiles, 2002, p. 8.)

Hiles, then, posits that the human mind understands through narrative, through making a story out of events. If we try to eschew this "narrative intelligence", we will be cutting ourselves off from a foundational pathway towards knowledge and meaning. We risk being blocked because our understanding is prematurely curtailed. The more we know, the more we can write and the more fluently we can write. Of course, it's not always easy to work out which is the first step in the merry dance between language, narrative, self-concept and world-view. Afterall, words are invented, language develops, in order to embrace changes in the way we see ourselves and the community within which we live. Narratives alter. Do we need the words to alter the narrative, or will the imperative of the narrative force us to find the words which express the new? For my purposes, it's not necessary to have a firm view on how language and narrative and the construction of meaning interlink, just to bear in mind that there are some sorts of causal connections. As Taylor (1989) suggests, we understand our worlds through narrative, we are inescapably in the narrative.

Summary Box

Humans acquire knowledge through narrative, through describing events and setting them into a pattern. Our narrative skills are important in gaining scholarly understanding. An enhanced capacity to comprehend will ease our writing.

THE NARRATIVE OF OURSELVES AS WRITERS

I am a writer. It has taken me some time to fully own that title. I am imagining that many of the readers of this book do not view themselves as writers. How do they view themselves? As someone who hates, or struggles, to write? As a competent but basically uninspired writer? As someone who rarely makes the grade when writing? Perhaps you are a supervisor who is comfortable with their own status as writer, but is trying to support someone who has a very low opinion of their writing skills? Where do we get our notions about ourselves as writers from? They will come from past experiences and from what people have said about us and our work. We will remember some of these (and not others) and fit them into a narrative. For example,

CHAPTER 4

my remedial reading classes at the age of eight or nine and my initial struggle to establish myself as a writer gives me a narrative of effort and of overcoming obstacles. Included in my narrative is a trepidation at taking on the designation of writer, knowing that people's first question would be, "And where can I buy your books?" — when these books were still unpublished.

The narrative of the self is always in the making. There are new experiences; for example, praise for my articles makes my claim to be a writer stronger. Or, perhaps, there are reassessments of the past: my years of not being published are a valid apprenticeship which makes me a better writer today.

> The realization of self as a narrative in process serves to gather what one has been, in order to imagine what one will be and to judge whether this is what one wants to become. Life is not merely a story text: life is lived and the story is told. The life story is a redescription of the lived life and a means to integrate the aspects of the self. (Polkinghorne, 1988, p. 154.)

Have we created a narrative of ourselves which does not recognise, or undervalues that part of us which writes? Would re-evaluating our narrative give a more secure sense of ourselves as writers? Do we discount, for example, when we do write well? Do we take enough notice of when we are praised for what we have produced? Do we underplay our ability to tell stories because we're more adroit orally than in writing? Can we augment what we already believe about ourselves as writers with some more positive observations? In Case Study 4, being allowed to use a word processor in exams meant George produced some "competent pieces of work" which he was "proud of". The new technology was able to take on the burden of the mechanics of getting the words onto the paper, meaning that George could concentrate on style and composition and he achieved something he was proud of. Could he now fold this into his narrative and acknowledge some of his skills as a writer?

In Chapter 2 I have already suggested that writing is a relational act: we write in order to say something to somebody. In this chapter, drawing on Hiles (2002) and Polkinghorne (1988), I have proposed that narrative is what binds people together, creates understandings within societies and cultures. Writing narrative, therefore, is one way in which we as humans reach out and make connections with other human beings. In Chapter 3, I explored more fully the concept of "attachment" to express how we relate to others and the world around us. To briefly summarise here, some of us will be comfortable with close attachments to others, some of us will be less easy and will want to avoid intimate connections. Consultant psychiatrist/psychotherapist Jeremy Holmes (2008, p. 3), has found that our "attachment" inclinations may affect how we are able to tell a story. He says, "Attachment theory suggests that there are classic ways of not telling a story — in the service of defending against mental pain." He proposes that someone who avoids relationships defends themselves by resorting to cliché, thus avoiding having to tell their individual take on a story. Someone who is insecure or distrustful in their relationships may have a fragile hold on their narrative, not being able to put it in an order that works for them or ending up with too many hanging threads.

It is possible that these proclivities in personal storytelling could spill out into how someone approaches narrative-making in general. Hence their academic writing becomes cliché driven or jumbled and dislocated. On the other hand, also in Chapter 3, I make a case for writing being an activity we can attach to in itself, even when we find our connectedness to other parts of our life more fraught. This being the potential of writing (encouraged via, for instance, the writing journal introduced in Chapter 1), the activity of putting words onto the paper and our absorption in it can also be a counterbalance to Holmes's "classic ways of not telling a story" which may be encountered orally. We can train ourselves to overcome our usual disrupted narrative creation through writing.

> We are the sole survivors of a world no-one else has seen.
> (John le Carré)

We are the only people who can write this essay or this thesis in this particular way. We are the only ones who can put our own unique personal spin on it. Yet the place for the individual as author, for an authentic voice, within academic writing depends on the conventions of the discipline. It is also a point of discussion, especially between those who broadly see themselves as qualitative and those who consider themselves quantitative researchers. I return to this variance and discussion in Chapter 5. Here I want to make the link between these conventions and our own personal narrative. Perhaps we see ourselves as a shy person with nothing outstanding to say; that is our story about ourselves. If we are then being asked in our academic writing to reveal our personal authorship, this may be difficult for us. While someone who wants to be noticed, such as my Case Study 1, might feel sunk into insignificance in amongst an alien language which is "constraining", "incoherent", merely a "rehashing" of someone else's words.

Our own personal narrative concerning us as an academic writer might clash with how we perceive academic writers ought to be. It could lead to the "imposter syndrome" developed in more depth in Chapter 2. The point here is to consider how our own personal narrative of ourselves as writer within the academic environment might clash with the rules and culture of the academic world or, at least, our perceptions of them.

Summary Box

We all have our own narrative concerning whether we consider ourselves to be a writer and, if we do, what kind of writer. This narrative has been constructed from past experiences. It is still being constructed. It is open to rewriting, editing and re-assessment which can help us to feel more comfortable taking on the role of writer.

CHAPTER 4

WRITING BLOCKS

We have visited three aspects of narrative:

- Storytelling being a natural impulse for us as human beings.
- Narrative as a way of finding meaning and developing understandings.
- Our own personal narrative concerning whether we see ourselves as writers or not.

These are the three narrative planets I have set spinning in the writing block universe. Now I want to explore how their gravitational pulls stay our writing hands.

We all have a propensity for storytelling. However, hedged in by its conventions and expectations, we may forget this when we tackle our academic writing. The idea that our essay or thesis may have anything in common with the tale we told our supervisor about why we haven't turned in our latest draft on time may seem fantastical. And yet, approaching our academic pieces as if they were something other, more complex perhaps, less intuitive, can block us from writing.

Narrative — putting events into sequence, looking for linkages, having a sense of temporality — aids us in comprehending experiences and ideas. By ignoring this method of gaining knowledge, which Hiles (2002) has suggested is "a basic property of the human mind", we risk being blocked because we have not grasped what it is we are attempting to understand. In addition, in the academic world, what we are engaged in may be very complex: it's hard to find the words to express the subtleties of everything we want to say. We may be faced with competing perspectives. As Polkinghorne (1988, p. 26) puts it:

> [D]espite the attempt to create an ideal language for formal science, there remains a gap between the categories of any language and those of objective reality... [therefore] the philosophic enterprise should turn away from the inquiry into ultimate truths and toward participation in conversation.

Telling the story allows us a way into this multi-faceted academic world, with each part of the "conversation" being presented as a different narrative. Think of the many modern novels where each chapter is told by a different character picking away at what are essentially the same events. This is one way into this multi-layered, multiperspective academic writing.

Finally, we have our own personal narrative which may block us. Do we accept that we can write? Or is our story that we cannot write, do not have the "gift" given to everyone else, as George in Case Study 4 describes it? In our own personal story, do we feel we belong in the academic world? Or do we feel an "imposter"? Our personal narrative is open to being added to or being remade and reassessed; we do have the opportunity to free our writing hand by recognising some of the skills we do have as a writer.

WRITING STRATEGIES

Some of what's already been said about story-making and academia and our own personal story-making may have freed up the writing hand sufficiently to get you going again. Since storytelling is intuitively oral, speaking the narrative of your academic work to a supervisor or trusted colleague could be a starting point for finding the story. This could be recorded and then transcribed. You now have words on the paper which are set in a sequence and can be worked with, fitted into the requirements of the academic piece you are producing.

Writing or telling your own personal writing story can also be liberating; again it can be shared with someone who is empathic and supportive. Along the way, notice if there are other interpretations to the ones you have made. Are there things you have given too much weight to and others which you have discounted? Would it be possible to reassess experiences or bring in others that would support your role as an academic writer? Could others — peers, friends, tutors, supervisors — contribute to this process of reconfiguring your narrative? In Evans (2011, p. 181) my interviewee talked about doing this:

> The narrative-making, the telling it, and also recognising it, and every time I tell it I recognise other bits about it, that actually helps me to move forward.

Through telling our own story, we can discover the forgotten storyteller who likes nothing better than to draw people near with their richly constructed tales. We can get in touch with the academic who is able to use their capacity as a storyteller to create meaning and understandings which they can than communicate effectively to others.

Stories help us to get in touch with our material, giving us access to it, so that we are then able to mould it given the proscriptions of the academic writing we are working within. And yet, even academic writing is a narrative, so thinking of it as a story with a plot and characters may still help. Stories have a particular shape to them. For instance, the quest story (which is the basic outline of most), transfers quite easily into a lot of academic writing. First there is the statement of the quest (or question for the essay, thesis chapter or article). Then the movement through the journey of exploration with, generally, three obstacles being thrown in the way of the quester (these could be, for example, three problems resolved during the research, or three theories to be countered). The quester has their own champions/helpers who come in during this stage (perhaps supportive theories or research results). Then a resolution is found when the quest is restated and the result of the journey described.

This chapter fits into this quest template. My quest was to fit ideas around narrative to writing blocks. I visited the three aspects of narrative I wanted to explore in turn using supportive theories and references. I then linked each of the three with blocks to writing, finally offering possible routes through. In taking a plot outline, it is sometimes useful to start with the headings; for example, quest, first obstacle/theory, second obstacle/theory etc. Headings can always be changed later to fit in with the academic conventions you are working within.

Frank (1995) found that when people became seriously ill, they graduated towards three basic narratives: chaos; restitution and quest. The first is that the

CHAPTER 4

illness has turned the person's world upside down and it will never be right or righted again. The second is that despite the illness the person will return to how they were before its onslaught. The third is that illness necessitates (and can also be seen as an opportunity for) the person to search out and discover new ways of being. Again these basic templates of narrative may fit our interpretation of our material and guide us into the story we want to tell. Is ours a narrative of chaos, of restitution or of quest?

Fairy Tales

There are "stories so old they don't even *have* writers". (Le Guinn, 2004, p. 109.) They come from our oral tradition of storytelling. We might call them myths or legends or fairy tales. I like the latter term, even though it has its downsides. Fairy tales conjure up the sanitised versions which are available in every children's library or via Disney animation. They were mostly gathered together and written down in the Europe of the nineteenth century, which means that they carry with them many of the mores and values of that time and that region in that time. Being written down, they also lost the most compelling aspect of fairy tales, that each teller makes up their own version. Suddenly we received a version which was immutable because it was set down in printed type. Fairy tales, folk tales, have always been told and retold, adapted to changing circumstances. Among their aims have been that of helping humans to make sense of their world and that of passing on information and wisdom about how to live.

Fairy tales, when we go back to their very basics, are quests, are journeys. They deal with the big existential issues: of our purpose, of life, of death, of hate, of love. In today's society we are more used to thinking about the struggle between good and evil being internal rather than being between the forces of the righteous against the might of the wicked. However, our sense of there being a tussle, a conflict, in whatever field we are working in may well be applicable. We can say that there are forces at work which meet, clash and mould one another in many different ways. In fairy tales there are protagonists, there are obstacles, there are helpers, there is movement, there is conflict, there is some kind of resolution. The magic is merely that which we still do not know.

Fairy tales can give us a framework on which to hang our own story, which can help us to see it with greater clarity and, therefore, express it with more precision. In the end, we will have to fit it into certain academic structures, which won't allow us to explicitly use fairy-tale language to say what we have to say. However, finding the story through a fairy tale could give us the impetus and insight to get to our desired end result.

Before embarking on these exercises please read the section "Read This First!" in the introduction to this book. Remember not to spend too much time on each one, notice what you have written rather than judge it and, if possible, share what you are discovering with a supportive peer or supervisor.

An exercise with fairy tales — getting going Choose your favourite fairy tale. Or if you haven't read a fairy tale in a goodly while, seek some out, preferably some in the original brothers Grimm versions, or perhaps some folk tales from cultures and countries other than your own.

Once you have a story in mind, write down its essential elements. These questions might help you:

– Who is the main protagonist?
– What is the main protagonist's main preoccupation?
– What stands in the way of the main protagonist and their main preoccupation?
– Who is there to help the main protagonist?
– How does the main protagonist get what they want?
– What's the emotional tone of the ending?
– What's the message carried by the story?

Try one or two of these:

– Do some "free"[1] writing, using the message as a starting point.
– Write from the protagonist's point of view, looking back as a person near the end of their life.
– Write from the point of view of someone observing the action.
– Write from the point of view of an inanimate object; for example, a clock, or the protagonist's cloak, or the walls of a dwelling.

Can you identify a link between the writer-in-you or your research material and the protagonist, the protagonist's preoccupation or the message of the tale? Write a short piece exploring this.

Red Riding Hood comes to my mind. I have always been fascinated by the wolf within.

The Meaning of Wolves by Kate Evans

> Everybody knows the story —
> the harmless little girl,
> the harmless old granny —
> but everyone knows: adults lie.
>
> And Grandma grew
> her snout and fine set of gnashers
> out of her own mouth
> for the wolf always lived in her tummy,
> and the more she denied his burping,
> the more persistent he became,
> until, well, she even gobbled up her own granddaughter.
>
> And you can weigh down your wolf's skin
> with as many stones as you like
> but that won't stop it
> rising to the surface again.

CHAPTER 4

An exercise with fairy tales — our writing story   Again you can choose your own fairy tale, or perhaps this one:

> A young person is bereaved; one of their parents is dead. Unfortunately, their surviving parent decides to marry again and their step-parent and stepsiblings are cruel and uncaring. Our protagonist is desperate to achieve their goal (perhaps write an essay/thesis/article/book). Three times they try, three times their stepfamily members put other tasks in their way. They feel hopeless, but help is on hand. With this aid, our protagonist does make it partly to where they want to be. But once more their ambition is cruelly cut off. They are distraught. Now, what can happen for them to finally reach their glittering prize?

Use the framework from your story, or the one sketched above, to write about your own story as a writer. Start as early as you can go back. What or who was it that stopped you in your tracks? Who or what are your "ugly" stepfamily? What are their motivations and what do you need to counter them? What has to happen for you to reach your glittering prize?
Or try this story thread:

> Your quest is to be an academic writer. You have lost the capacity to tell stories, though you had it once,. Write about what it was like when you wrote fluently, when words dripped from your lips like mango juice. Now write what it is like to be dry and bereft. What three things get in the way of your writing? Then magically you are at your desk, writing and writing; the words roll easily across the screen of your computer or the page of your notebook. What is that like? Describe it. Finally, the clock strikes midnight. You leave your work to go to bed. But the next morning you find it has all gone. What has happened to it? How are you going to get it back?

An exercise with fairy tales — our research material
> The boy has found a gold key
> and he is looking for what it will open.
> This boy!
> Upon finding a nickel
> he would look for a harp.
> Therefore he holds the key tightly.
> (Sexton, 1971, p. 2.)

Holding our research topic — or a part of it — or some aspect of the material we are working on in mind, does a fairy tale suggest itself? Beginning with, "Once upon a time…" start to write it from the point of view of the main protagonist or from the point of view of a disinterested observer. Carry on writing as freely as you can for about five minutes.

Another starting point could be the metaphor of keys which comes into many fairy tales. You have a key. Describe it. It's been lost. Who has lost it? You have found it. Where? How? You have made a journey — describe that journey — to a dwelling. Describing the place you have found yourself in, you discover a trunk. What do you hope to find inside? However, as you approach the trunk, the trunk's protector appears and gives you three tasks before you can access the treasure you seek. Write about these tasks and the final moment when you open your trunk with your key.

Approaching our academic subjects through fairy tales may give us new insights which keep us writing. Or we may already have all the material we need and just don't know how to structure it. The academic constructions seem daunting and baffling. The more familiar fairy tale configuration can give us a framework, a template, on which to hang our work. The fairy tale plot can assist us in finding the story underlying our essay, or chapter in our thesis. It can also help us re-fabric our writing story, thus giving us greater ease with our writing skills.

CONCLUSION

> However we may analyse or try to explain it, the power of a good story is a primitive, irreducible mystery that answers to some need deep in human nature. (Swift, 2009, p. 12.)

We are all storytellers, we have imbibed stories from young. Storytelling is an important element in the way humans construct understanding and disseminate it. It is also crucial in terms of how we gain a sense of who we are. We tell stories about ourselves and listen to other people's stories about us and form opinions about our capacities; for instance, our capacity to write academically.

We become blocked when our storytelling potential becomes stymied on tackling our academic writing. The conventions and style of essay- or thesis-writing give us the impression that this is something other than the narratives we are used to. We eschew the story plotlines we are familiar with — the description of events and the search for consequential linkages — and become overwhelmed in trying to search out something more. Or we ignore the meaning which comes out of narrative-making, comes out of, in other words, finding the pattern within ideas or happenings as we string them together. Or our own story of us as an academic writer closes us down and undermines our confidence in our skills. These three aspects to narrative can cause us to become blocked.

On the other hand, our own innate story-making and remaking impulse can unblock us. It can offer the coherent structure we need to get us started. It can assist in creating the meaning we need to keep going. And it can give a different perspective on how we perceive ourselves as writers, thus giving us permission to write more freely.

CHAPTER 4

Narrative — the key to your academic writing

NOTE

1. See "Writing Strategies" in Chapter 1.

CHAPTER 5

ACADEMIC WRITING: NEW APPROACHES

*Conventions and New Approaches in Academic Writing —
How They Impact Writing Blocks*

We find before us a new terrain, hardly trodden by those who have come before. We set our toe across the border and wonder. Is this private property? Dare we go further? It looks inviting though the ground is somewhat uneven. We are excited and filled with trepidation. This is unchartered, unmapped. We could be the first to discover it. We place our foot firmly over the boundary expecting an immediate wail of sirens or storm of security guards. Nothing. We see faint traces of other steps going off in many directions. Still there is enough room for us to choose to follow or to find our own route. We take a breath and then walk forward slowly.

INTRODUCTION

In this chapter I intend to explore how conventions and new approaches in academic writing influence our facility to write. It is difficult to imagine a scholarly activity which would not require some writing at some point. However, though humans may be natural storytellers (see Chapter 4), writing involves skills which can be acquired. How well we write depends on how we are introduced to, and encouraged to develop, the skills required. All writing has conventions and academic writing is no different. They too need to be appropriated and then given scope to flourish. Becoming more comfortable with academic writing is in part a question of engaging with a creative process (see Chapter 1) and in part a question of acquiring capacities and then being supported in advancing and expanding on them. If we find our writing blocked, is it because we need to build up the skills necessary? Or progress those we already have? This chapter discusses how the conventions within academic writing might affect our proficiency as writers.

I will be considering:

- Writing's pivotal role in academia.
- The conventions in academic writing and their evolution.
- Writing blocks.
- Writing strategies.

CHAPTER 5

WRITING'S PIVOTAL ROLE IN ACADEMIA

Writing holds a central place within academia, both as a means of communication and as a means of assessment. A browse through a university library will reveal numerous titles which show the emphasis put on being able to write. Hamp-Lyons and Heasley (2006); Jordan (1999); Brewer (2007); Dunleavy (2003); Woods (1999); and Redman (2001) are but a very few of those on offer. Holloway (2005, p. 271) quoting Alasuutari (1995), emphasises the weight given to writing in qualitative research. "[W]riting is the most important part of the research. When all is said and done, the world is left with nothing else but the text." This significance given to the written word also came through my interviews with people from non-qualitative, non-human-science worlds. "What makes a good biochemist?" said one senior lecturer. "Good writing is essential." Both for students — "You may know it but if you can't write it down we can't assess it," and in general — "You can't get far in science if you can't write; you have to write your papers, your grant proposals, your theses."

George (Case Study 4) has just completed his first year on a general science degree. During his final years at school he had avoided subjects which required any extended writing. He was nonplussed, therefore, to discover that his degree required him to produce essays. He describes what it's like for him, beginning with his previous experience of writing essays: "You spend ages on it and at the end of the day you finally produce a piece of work and it comes back covered in red pen. And I think that's why at 'A' Level I thought, I never want to be assessed on these subjects again. And it's interesting at university when, even in a science degree, you have to do that kind of extended writing and you have to readjust and really get back into the original stuff that you thought you were rubbish at."

The number of books on the subject not only underlines the importance of writing in academia, it also suggests that academic writing is about skills which can be taught and, therefore, acquired (Antoniou and Moriarty, 2008). This requires application and can be tough going (Woods, 1999; Wellington, 2010). Support may be variable, or those in need of it may not avail themselves of it for a range of reasons including time, inclination and reasons of affect (see Chapter 2).

George describes some of the extended writing expected of him: "We did book reviews on popular science writing; which was pretty good, I really enjoyed the books but I don't know, it just didn't flow for me. I mean, obviously it's not a massive issue for me because those two won't count, but I don't know, it feels a bit weird that you're going into a module with the expectation that you're probably not going to do as well as you'd hoped to. You may try, but it's quite difficult to find the motivation. As hard as you try for this, it'll probably never be as good as you anticipate or want it to be; you're kind-of resigning yourself to mediocrity from the start."

On the other hand, with time, with support, with motivation, writing skills can be attained and they can flourish. How much we choose to do this will depend on our long-term aims. To become adequate at essay writing will obviously take less effort than if we want to find enough facility in writing to produce a thesis, articles or a book.

> **Summary Box**
>
> Writing is important in academia. It is one of the foremost ways that we communicate to each other. It is also a way that we are assessed, and, therefore, it is crucial to our progression. However, writing is not something that comes naturally to anyone. It is something we all learnt to do and then practise and develop as far as is appropriate to our context.

THE CONVENTIONS IN ACADEMIC WRITING AND THEIR EVOLUTION

All genres or types of writing have their own history, traditions and conventions. Academic writing is no different (Wellington, 2010; Ivanič, 1998). Since in writing we are using squiggles on a page to communicate, there has to be some agreement as to how these squiggles should be interpreted. Conventions help to clarify this agreement within different contexts. They assist with understanding and with our human interchange. Imagine trying to follow this paragraph without the aid of full stops and commas; in other words, the conventions of punctuation.

The conventions associated with academic writing vary from field to field, so as novice writers we need to find out what they are for our own particular discipline via, for instance, lecturers, study guides, books, websites. The rules can also be more nuanced than at first glance. For example, the divergence between some scientific subjects and some qualitative research writing may be more apparent than actual. The convention for much scientific writing is that the "I" of the author disappears behind a passive voice — "This was done" rather than "I did this". There is a tendency towards eschewing uncertainty and focusing on what, by agreement, have been designated as facts. On the other hand, for some qualitative research subject areas it is the active, first-person, uncertain writing which is definitely preferred. However, the biochemists I interviewed gave a different slant. Initially they said that the writing for their discipline is not meant to have "a personality", that the content is meant to be very neutral and that the "'I' disappears". They then went on to say, "In reality, we may be grasping after something. What everyone knows is that though we're presenting it in a logical way, that's not how it happens. We purify it all; it's artificial in some ways. In the end it is an edifice of best guesses." The convention itself has layers: on the surface the "I" is absent and certainty is the focus; however, it is recognised that underneath there is an uncertain "I" behind what is being written.

Trying to find our way round the conventions of academic writing may cause some of us to come to a halt. The conventions themselves, however, may lead to writing being blocked. Some of us may find the passive voice a difficult technique to handle or we struggle to express our own thoughts through it. Conversely, the use of the bold "I" may feel too exposing or self-aggrandising for others. Unfortunately, as one senior lecturer in biochemistry put it, "There are a hell of a lot of conventions in science which you have to absorb as you go along but which might be difficult to

CHAPTER 5

articulate clearly." For those steeped in academia, the conventions in their particular field will have become like the wallpaper in their office, hardly worth noticing any more; whereas for those coming in, they might appear shifting, spurious and unknowable.

The Evolution of Conventions in Academic Writing

As with any other genre, the conventions within academic writing evolve. This is a continual progression in order to respond to our changing understanding of knowledge and of our role as researchers. Academia does not stand still and this is mirrored in its writing, both in terms of method and of the way language is used. How, why and what we research, and then how we choose to disseminate our new understandings, changes over time. The conventions may mirror, lead or follow social, political, cultural and philosophical movements which are unfolding. Academia is not an impregnable ivory tower, but, on the contrary, it is inexorably interwoven into the fabric of the social world within which it exists (Wellington, 2010).

The rules of academic writing are not static. They bend and mould as our approaches to knowledge and research shape, and are themselves reshaped by, the social and philosophical context within which we find ourselves. It is an ongoing, fluid threading between, around and together which adds colour and vibrancy to our writing. The opposite of this, a rigid sticking to what has gone before, just because that is what has been done before, and a lack of interaction with our context, can lead to writing which expires in its own dullness. Without this evolution of conventions we may find ourselves stymied because we cannot express the developing academic environment within which we find ourselves. We need this evolution, then, to keep us writing.

An example of a developing context which requires the evolution of academic writing conventions is the ongoing critique of the "scientific method". A full examination of this would be way beyond the scope of this book; however, I want to highlight two aspects in brief summary:

– The existence of many truths.
– The co-creation of research.

The existence of many truths There is a movement within academia towards a postmodernist context where the existence of doubt is acknowledged and the seeking of multiple perspectives has become more focal than the seeking of one truth (see, for example, Woods, 1999; Denzin & Lincoln, 2000; Richardson, 2000).

Social constructionalists, such as Kenneth Gergen (Gergen, 2012), state that, since language is a socially agreed construct in itself, there can be no value-neutral description, there is no universal truth. For Gergen, social constructionism is a verb, it's a way of doing, rather than a dogma. It is not about saying my way is better than yours, rather an acknowledgement of multiplicity and a question about how we reconcile the multiple realities. And crucially for my purposes, it invites creativity, it requires a more creative language. Ward (2011, p. 356) suggests that "socially constructed dichotomies/ dualisms." such as "art and science", "fact and fiction", "objective and subjective" and "detached and evocative" have held sway since the seventeenth century but have been challenged particularly in the last three decades of the twentieth.

A multiplicity of perspectives and room for doubt, for uncertainty and for liminality, are all aspects of a postmodernist academia which touches many disciplines. Though these are more associated with qualitative research in the human sciences, Sir Paul Nurse, geneticist and biologist who won the Nobel Prize in Physiology or Medicine in 2001, has spoken about how science is tentative and research must contain the notion of doubt (Nurse, 2012). Malterud (2001, p. 399) writing in *The Lancet* suggests that qualitative research, with its greater capacity for embracing the postmodernist context, should be working hand-in-hand with quantitative research in areas where the latter has traditionally predominated.

> Qualitative and quantitative studies should be thought of as being complementary rather than conflicting. Medical researchers need a broad range of research skills to choose the path of inquiry that will most adequately provide valid accounts of the actual study field. No methodology can in itself warrant scientific quality — the crucial condition is how the process of knowledge aggregation and organisation is handled and presented.

The co-creation of research   Very much linked to this multi-truth, multi-perspective approach is the idea that the researcher, the observer, the writer co-creates what is presented. This may be, for example, in terms of selection or interpretation of what is reported. Others (for example, Romanyshyn, 2007; Finlay, 2011) have postulated the relationship between the researcher and the researched further, and suggested that it is more complex and more crucial than is generally accepted within the traditional scientific method. They have conceptualised how the intertwining between researcher and the researched impacts one upon the other, eliciting response and then counter-response. This is also explored under the section on "parallel process" in Chapter 3.

The evolution of the academic context requires that the conventions of academic writing also become remodelled, that new approaches be sought and found. One aspect advocated by, for instance, Antoniou & Moriarty (2008) is that the split between academic and creative writing should be allowed to diminish, as it is "a relic of Western Enlightenment thought" and belongs to another academic era. Hence the creative approaches to writing advocated later in this chapter and also throughout this book.

Summary Box

As with any genre of writing, academic writing has its own conventions and rules. These conventions may be obvious or obscure, clear-cut or nuanced; they may suit our personal writing style or they may not. As the academic environment evolves, as new methods and philosophical underpinnings come to be embraced, so the conventions of academic writing become remodelled.

CHAPTER 5

WRITING BLOCKS

Writing blocks may occur because we are confused or overwhelmed by the conventions that govern academic writing. We don't know how to move from our jumble of thoughts and ideas (Chapter 1), from the narrative we have cobbled together (Chapter 4) to a fully fledged essay, article, thesis chapter, report. The conventions that govern these types of academic writing appear difficult and alien. Or else they do not suit us, they ask us to be bold in our assertions, or perhaps they ask us to hide ourselves away. We feel we will never get the hang of them and this stops us from writing. Furthermore, we may find ourselves in a shifting academic paradigm, where, for example, multiple perspectives are called for or our role as researcher requires examining, and we do not feel we have the language which is equal to this. The conventions may impede us, but, equally, the need to remould them, to find new approaches to communicating our work, could also bring us to a halt.

As already noted, there are as many different conventions as there are academic disciplines and forms in which academic writing appears. There are two aspects peculiar to academic writing, however, which may be particularly blocking:

– The peer review.
– Plagiarism.

The Peer Review

As already noted in previous chapters[1], feedback is essential for our creative process and for us to develop our writing. Yet with academic writing, it is rare to receive "friendly" feedback which is unadulterated by some form of (or perception of) assessment. This is incredibly damaging to a novice writer and to anyone who is developing their writing skills (in other words, all of us who dare to write, for we are always becoming).

Just the thought that we are being judged may be enough to stop us from writing. On the other hand, and I have come across this from a number of sources, the unowned, partial response of the peer review of academic articles appears to be particularly difficult to deal with. It can mean that someone never attempts to write an article in the first place, or it may result in them giving up in the face of the peer review they actually receive.

In Chapter 2, I look at how those involved in peer reviewing can be facilitating rather than blocking. Furthermore, later in this chapter I suggest that feedback can be effectively given in writing groups for academics. Though these may not take away the initial sting of a very critical peer review, they may support the author in moving forward with the feedback they have been given.

Plagiarism

Of course, plagiarism is a concern for all writers, but it is a particularly weighty issue for academic ones. I am not here to encourage or even excuse plagiarism or the contravening of copyright. On the other hand, paying homage, intertextuality and making allusions to, are all close cousins of plagiarism, which have found credence within poetry, drama, fiction and creative non-fiction. It is academics who are manifestly sensitive to any whiff of plagiarism. And could this be a stumbling block for some novice writers?

> Instead of viewing (plagiarism) as a crime prompting moral outrage one should, perhaps, view student writers' practices of lifting phrases wholesale from their reading as one of the consequences of their desire to identify with the academic discourse community. (Ivanič, 1998, p. 330.)

Ivanič is suggesting that the academic conventions themselves hedge students in so much that they fear not getting the language right and hence plagiarise. I also heard this from the biochemist lecturers I interviewed. They said that in science subjects there was the added anxiety that by using different words or phrases we might also be changing the meaning of a definition or theorem. A fear of "getting it wrong" within the academic paradigm leads to plagiarism; a fear of plagiarism leads to writing being blocked. By dealing openly with these fears, especially amongst students, writing blocks can be addressed.

Summary Box

We all need conventions to write in any genre. However, the apparently weighty conventions in academia — especially the peer review and plagiarism — may stop us from writing, either because they appear too overwhelming or because they do not suit us. In addition, new approaches may be needed for us to be able to communicate what it is we need to say..

WRITING STRATEGIES

Academic writing has conventions which at times can appear obstructively hidden or nuanced to the novice. The conventions are and need to be evolving, which may feed into a sense of not knowing quite what is expected, which can be blocking, or, on the other hand, could be freeing.

The first writing strategy must be to gather as much information as you can about the conventions which apply in your discipline. You are maybe working within an environment where it appears that everyone writes with ease or where it is assumed that the conventions and the mechanics of writing are picked up along the way, almost through osmosis. And that anyone who fails to do this is somehow lacking. This is not so: all writers have to serve an apprenticeship, have to develop their skills, have to learn the conventions of their particular field. All writers have to apply themselves to their writing.

CHAPTER 5

> Potential authors may not want to merely do things right (write a couple of letters and book reviews before trying some joint-authored pieces while assiduously following editorial guidelines); they believe in doing the right thing: writing brilliantly, as leaders in the field, from the outset. There seems a preference for art over craft: as if learning how to write is a stage to be avoided. (Newnes & Jones, 2005.)

Being in an atmosphere where the writing of essays, reports, articles, chapters is presented as something which is naturally acquired does make it hard to ask for support or guidance. Yet this support and guidance abounds. Books such as Redman's *Good Essay Writing* (2001) suggest good practice, for example:

- Make sure you understand what is being asked of you, especially in terms of the meanings of the words in any essay title you have been given.
- Consider if an essay title can be "chunked", ie split into sub-headings. For instance, "Discuss how the conventions in academic writing cause writing blocks" could already give rise to the sections: "What is academic writing?" "What conventions are there?" "How do they affect the facility to write?"
- Take into consideration any guidance notes from tutors and study advice services or feedback on previous work.
- Amass (Chapter 1) information messily before thinking about any logical order. For instance, one of my correspondents described starting on a final assessment: "I wrote down everything that I knew from my notes and things I must not forget on big wallpaper pieces. I hadn't a word count as such; however, I did feel that I'd taken a small step and had some words to work on." Then use post-its or cards with potential headings on and shuffle until the possible logical order presents itself.
- After the messy stage of the creative process (see Chapter 1), plan, draft and then rewrite. The introduction will probably be the last piece you finalise.

Sometimes it is a very simple suggestion gleaned from another — like, if you've got a thousand words and four topics, aim to write two hundred and fifty words on each — which keeps us rolling. This example comes from an editorial director of the *New York Times,* John Darnton (2001, p. xii), when he was writing his first novel:

> Soon I discovered a little gimmick. One day I complained to a friend and author, a fellow "hack" from the Nairobi press corps, that the work was going slowly, that I had been writing only a thousand words a day. He sat up like a bolt, downed his scotch and peered at me through a cloud of cigarette smoke. "One thousand words a day! That's terrific! Don't you realize? That's thirty thousand words a month. Three, four months and you've a book." I did the math; he was right. I set my computer so that I could knock off the moment I hit a thousand words. The device worked. A momentous task had been cut down to bite sizes. No longer was I laboring to climb a mountain while staring at the snow-covered peak far above; instead I was climbing a single slope day after day until one day I would arrive at the summit. And one day I did.

Writing, especially when it is given the central role it has in academia, can seem daunting. It is through talking about it and learning from others that we find our way up our own hills to reach our own high points.

I am a writer and a lover of writing; on the other hand, even I can see that there may be some aspects to academia which do not need to rely on written assessments. Are we perhaps too quick to use writing as a way to measure our own and others' skills? Could we be more open to other formats, other ways of showing knowledge, skills and acumen? Is this a discussion worth having with a supervisor or a tutor?

Knowing that rules exist, being cognisant of their variables and getting as much guidance on them as possible are good starting points. It can also help to consider how the conventions meet or contradict our own personal values or attitudes to writing. A contradiction could lead to us finding it hard to write. Bringing that into the open, perhaps through discussion, even if we finally have to accept that the conventions have to be abided by, could free us up.

On the other hand, I have also suggested that in order to keep writing, we may need to find new approaches which perhaps challenge some of the conventions in our discipline. Since the conventions in academic writing vary from discipline to discipline, the way, and the speed at which, academic writing develops and changes will also differ. It is worth exploring what is going on in your particular field through reading and discussion. As someone writing within academia, it is possible to both follow and contribute to the adaptation of conventions even in very small ways. I want to focus on two developments here which have the potential to ease writing blocks:

– Writing groups for academics.
– Finding the poetics in academic writing.

Writing Groups for Academics

> The assumption persists that if you are an academic, you are automatically both able and willing to write. (Moore, 2003, p. 334.)

Delving back into the biographies of writers in any number of genres, from fiction to non-fiction, from poetry to drama, it is clear that writers need other writers. They need them for guidance, for critical feedback, for encouragement, for motivation. As academics, we know this in terms of other aspects of our work, but how often do we sit down with a colleague and talk about writing? Maybe it is because we don't consider ourselves to be writers? Other aspects of our selves appear more significant. We may consider that we are an "imposter" as far as writing goes (see Chapters 2 and 4). Yet we are writing, every working day, and writing holds a pivotal role in academia, both for conveying what we have to say and also in terms of our progression. So why not do as other writers do: get together with our peers and talk about writing? Time, I would imagine, is the biggest impediment. However, if we think about all the time we spend not writing but trying to, being stuck, frustrated,

CHAPTER 5

blocked, do we have the time not to build in an opportunity which could see the end of those wasted hours?

Writing groups can be face-to-face, they can be online, they can be an ongoing commitment or organised to see us through a particular project, they can be as simple as agreeing with a colleague to meet over a coffee and talk about writing for thirty minutes a week. There is no fixed format to which a writing group must conform, though here are two things to think about:

- The limits of the group.
- The role of feedback.

The limits of the group   What is the group going to be about? I would suggest that it should be about encouragement and about writing, the craft of writing, the process of writing (see Chapter 1) rather than necessarily about the content of what we are trying to communicate. This would mean that it could be a cross-discipline group which could be very rich indeed in terms of learning from each other.

> Instead of a solitary, isolated, solely competitive activity, it is more useful to approach [academic writing] as a community-based, collaborative, social act. (Moore, 2003, p. 334.)

Academia can be a competitive place. Participants in a writing group need to feel safe enough to be able to share what they find difficult, what they don't feel confident about. It would be important to find ways to ensure this, maybe through ground rules or perhaps by having a facilitator, at the very least by acknowledging that there might be a tension in not wanting to show our vulnerabilities to colleagues.

Reading is an important aspect of writing. Reading feeds into our writing; it can nourish and inform it. The senior lecturer in biochemistry I interviewed noted that students who read were better writers. She said, "It doesn't matter what they read; it could be novels, they write better because they absorb style and they absorb storytelling." So bringing in examples of good writing, whether it be from the academic realm or not, may be a safer way to get into the subject of writing than starting straight away with examples of our own.

It's also useful to get practical issues around group organisation discussed and agreed from the start. Who will be allowed to join? What will they be told about the aims of the group? What commitment will be expected of participants? These are a few questions worth asking; there will be others depending on circumstance and context.

The role of feedback   Feedback is a topic regularly chewed over at all writers' groups. When, how and by whom are useful starting points. I would urge that the authors themselves remain in control of the feedback they receive. It is good practice to ask specific questions of the people giving feedback so that they are forced into giving specific answers. For example, "Where is the language pitched right for an undergraduate audience?" Or, "Are there places where I could give more examples?"

Or pick out a paragraph where as an author your heart sinks or you become bored and ask for tips on that part only. People giving feedback should be requested to be specific, to offer ways forward and focus on the writing.

Authors should think carefully about when they want feedback. Too soon and the feedback could stymie any further work. Too late and it becomes irrelevant. I like to think about a piece of writing as a growing plant. Feedback too early is like having the shoot stamped on just as it peeps above ground. Too late and the bush is fully formed and clipped, all it wants is to be admired. Hard as it is, as writers (and this applies to writers in any genre) we need to get used to releasing our drafts.

> When someone reads your rough draft, it's like letting them see you half-dressed. It's about arriving at a level of intellectual comfort — or having faith in the process. In a successful collaboration, both people feel like they did less than half the work. (Writer Tim Requarth, in Morris, 2012)

And always, always risk asking: "What was good about this piece?"

I have enjoyed being part of different sorts of writing groups, finding them valuable and challenging in diverse ways. When I took on the project to write this book, I knew that feedback from those I usually relied on would not be as beneficial as it has been in the past because they were not immersed in the academic world. Luckily I was able to persuade a number of colleagues who know academia well to aid me in my endeavours. Knowing their heavy work burdens, I decided to divide up the tasks. Chapters were meted out. I asked them to spend no more than thirty minutes reading and thirty minutes responding. I then negotiated whether they would give me their responses in person or via email (or sometimes both). I knew the point at which I needed feedback: it was when I had a first draft and I was confident of the general shape and the basic content, but I had not read through it all myself more than once. I always asked specific questions. Here are some examples:

- What do you like about it?
- Are the links between creative writing techniques/authentic voice and writing blocks securely made or are there places where they need tightening?
- Do my examples work? Do they illustrate sufficiently what I am trying to put across?

Following the rewriting after this feedback, I sent the chapters to people who were perhaps less au fait with academia, but who I knew read a lot and could be a "fresh pair of eyes" before I completed my final version. These inputs, at different times and of varying tenors, have been crucial in keeping me motivated and my writing on track. For the final manuscript I asked someone qualified in the skill to do the proofreading. I do not believe that is something the author or people who have seen the text before can do effectively.

Writing groups amongst academics are not as common as amongst writers in other genres; however, they do exist and do show dividends (Moore, 2003; Murray, 2001; Lee & Boud, 2003). With some thought about their aims and how to manage the dynamics, they can be simple arrangements between peers and can be useful antidotes to writing blocks.

Finding the Poetics in Academic Writing

I'm not interested in making every academic a poet. I am interested in igniting interest amongst academics in the potential of poetic expression, and this includes within prose-writing. Why? Firstly, because, to meet the challenges of today's academia, we need language which can embrace "the provisional character of our knowing" (Romanyshyn, 2007, p. 27). A language which is "flexible" and "works creatively 'in the cracks', not just logically but metaphorically, poetically and evocatively." (Todres, 2007, p. 18.) A grasp of words which can "evoke and provoke understandings that traditional research formats cannot provide" (Sinner et al., 2006, p. 1224). Secondly because poetry and academic writing share a similarity in their continual search for meticulousness in detail and precision in choice of expression. Poetry is a digging-up, an excavation, as poet Seamus Heaney suggests (1984). It is, therefore, apposite for the revelatory aspects of academic work. And thirdly, because if we avail ourselves of the breadth of language accessible to us, then we are less likely to find we have become stumped for words.

> Ah! well for us, if even we,
> Even for a moment, can get free
> Our heart, and have our lips unchain'd;
> (Extract, Matthew Arnold "The Buried Life".)

Poetics and academic writing, such strange bedfellows: it cannot be? And yet it already is. The use of art-based creative techniques, including poetry, as method, in data analysis, in reflection, in presentation, is already happening. This quiet revolution is being led by educational researchers (Sinner et al., 2006) and those working in the health and social sciences and the humanities (Prendergast et al., 2009; Spencer, 2011; Adame et al., 2011). See also such events as the Warwick Medical School (UK) 2012 International Symposium on Poetry and Medicine, (www2.warwick.ac.uk/fac/med/research/csri/research/cpt/poetry/symp).

Richardson (2000, p. 925) argues that, given its conventions, all academic writing has an essential constructedness, which is overlaid by the "belief" that its words are "objective, precise, unambiguous, noncontextual and nonmetaphoric". Richardson suggests, however, that this "belief" is misplaced as "no textual staging is ever innocent … [or] neutral" (p. 925). Using more creative, more poetic language, we engage with a different type of constructedness, but one which is more obviously so and is more transparent about the writer's role. It is, therefore, more suited to the present academic context. And academics have begun to explore how the richness of the poetic language has allowed them to be opened up where their writing has become, or risks being, stifled (see: Jones, 2010; Ward, 2011; Spencer, 2006; Furman, 2006).

> [Creative techniques] evoke deep and powerful emotional reactions in the consumer of research. The expressive and creative arts seek to expand understanding, present subtle ideas that might even be paradoxical or dialectic, and lend themselves to the study of that which is difficult to reduce. (Furman, 2006, p. 561.)

In the way it can capture a "state of affairs" (Abbott, 2007, p. 69) — a moment, an image, an emotion — which is often too fleeting; in the way it can capture silences in its line or stanza breaks and the white space it can put around words; in the way it can capture the rhythm and speech patterns of our interviewees (Rapport, 2009): in all these ways, poetry and poetic prose are able to give us glimpses on which we can build and which could otherwise escape us. They also allow us to communicate these glimpses to others powerfully.

In doing all this, poetic language can assist us through writing blocks which occur because conventional academic language is too stultifying or constricting. It is important for me to clarify here that I do not want to whistle up memories of uninspiring class exercises to emulate the "great" poets, or of tortuous "Eng Lit" exams. This is far more free-flowing and playful.

> I am concerned that some researchers put poetry on a pedestal as an object for awe-inspiring reverence. I like to stress that poetry is earthy, rooted in everyday experience, connected integrally to the flow of blood in our bodies, expressed constantly in the rhythms of our speech and embodied movement. (Leggo, 2008, p. 170.)

The idea is not to create great poetry (however that might be defined, and poets argue about this endlessly) but to find a new way into our material. And then to present our insights in an engaging way for our readers. Since we ourselves are our own first reader, writing engagingly using poetic language can also assist with the continued flow of words.

Example: Case Study 2

When Sue hit a wall with her PhD, she went to some creative writing classes. She explains, "That's really when everything changed for me because I could write. It was only an hour workshop but I, you know, wrote. And from that experience I ended up writing poems from my data; and my PhD supervisor, you could just see her thinking, well, you've lost the plot now. The poetry that came out of the PhD is now on the Queen's Nursing Institute website for anybody to possibly come across, and I didn't ever stop myself thinking that was a bloody good idea. When the woman who runs the Queen's Nursing Institute said do it, I went, OK, I will. And I did. And they are not my best poems because they're the first poems that I wrote, and I wrote them six years ago, but I never once thought, 'Don't do it.' Because it gives a voice to those people who I interviewed."

CHAPTER 5

We could do something as simple as reading some poetry in an anthology or on-line. In doing this we can notice the ordinary-ness mixed with the richness of the language, how emphasis and pauses take their turn. It may encourage us to experiment with our own words and vocabulary. The poetry need not be in the final piece we choose to show to others; it might be, rather, a step in the writing process, to get us moving and sifting through our material in a way which can bring unexpected insights to the fore.

> a poem is
> this moment, the moment of writing with the quest, questing with the writing
> a bucket of berries
> holding tentatively instead of with tentacles
> yearning and learning to listen
> …
> a poem is
> caring about words
> a yearning for hinting at the ineffable
> a way of opening up a passage through the frozen tundra of the heart
> inscribing circles in the air that invite jumping through
> (Leggo, 2005, pp. 447, 454.)

Bringing poetic language into our academic writing may be a way of opening ourselves up, of breaking through a writing block caused by not finding the words to express what we have to say. How to do this? As Leggo suggests, it is about "caring about words" — their sounds, their meanings, their double and triple meanings. It is also about noticing the pauses which come between words, the moments of silence, of doubt. In poetic language these are expressed through line breaks, through white space on the page. It is about being playful with words and there is more on this in the next chapter.

In this chapter, I have introduced the idea that academia in a postmodern context may need to look for new approaches to express doubt, to give perspectives other than the author's own, to allow other voices to come through rather than have the author's predominate. This is especially true for people who are involved in qualitative interviewing. It may also assist in other disciplines, however, where there is a desire to acquire diverse insights into the topic under consideration. One possible new approach is "poetic transcription" or "poetic representation".

The conventions of qualitative academic writing already call for the use of quotations from interviewees. "Poetic transcription" (Prendergast, Leggo & Sameshima, 2009) is one way of "searching for the essence conveyed, the hues, the textures" letting us "know a person in a different way" (Glesne, quoted in Prendergast, Leggo & Sameshima, 2009, p. xxv).

Researcher Shinebourne (2011) explains her own technique for what she terms "poetic representation":

- Using only the participant's own words, but not necessarily in the same sequence as in the original interview.
- Extracting portions of the interview: evocative phrases, recurrent phrases, images and metaphoric descriptions which appeared particularly poignant in the context of the interview as whole.
- Significant segments of the interview were kept together to re-present the participant's speaking rhythm.
- The segments were repeatedly arranged and rearranged in a poetic form until a personally satisfactory Gestalt has been reached.
- As in all qualitative research, the sensibility of the researcher is implicated in the selection, interpretation and presentation of the material.

Shinebourne used this technique to present women's experience of alcohol addiction and recovery:

> Like there's a long well down in the ground
> Someone put me at the bottom
> I have to pull myself up brick by brick
> With my fingernails bleeding
> I cannot go back down there
> If I go back down there I'm dead.
> (Extract "I was going around with this mist in front of my eyes", Shinebourne, 2011.)

I followed a similar process to draw out themes from Case Study 2. Although I have been less strictly tied to the words of the transcript, here I have tried to represent in a graphic way the themes and the narrative of the interview. The word "chop" came up three times in the interview; however, only once in the sense that I have given it here. Yet it stayed with me when I was reflecting on the interview. It is an evocative, strong word and also put me in mind of the last line of the nursery rhyme *Oranges and Lemons*: "Here comes a chopper to chop off my head." The ragged line endings also aim to create a choppiness in the rhythm.

> Chop, chop, chop.
> Chop me up,
> burying the parts of me
> which are creative.
>
> Chop, chop, chop.
> Chop them up,
> those who have found voice
> and entrusted their words to me.

CHAPTER 5

> Cut them off again.
> Chop, chop, chop.
> Chop me down
> before I say too much —
> point out the difficult
> to swallow.
>
> Chop, chop, chop.
> Chop up the beast.
> It's chewed me up enough
> and there are other ways to say it.
> (Reflective piece by Kate Evans, based on the transcript of the interview with Sue, Case Study 2.)

Poetic transcription (or poetic representation) is one way of bringing us closer to the words and thought processes of another person. We can take on their voice and, therefore, in some ways, experience their perspective more fully. Additionally, poetic transcription or poetic representation can help us to focus on and distil down an aspect of what we want to say, from an interview, while also making connections with our own focus for our work. Powerfully and evocatively, poetic language allows us to touch another's perspective as well as what is essential in what we want to communicate. In these ways it is a route through when our writing is being stymied because we are overwhelmed by what needs to be said and we are searching round for the words adequate enough to say it.

CONCLUSION

In common with all writing, academic writing has its own conventions. These vary from discipline to discipline and, when working well, make it possible for us to communicate effectively and be assessed fairly. Writing blocks may occur because we are not clear about the conventions; or because we have not taken the time to learn the attendant skills, or sought the support, which would enable us to function proficiently within them. Writing blocks may also occur because our own personal values chafe against the rules or because the conventions are no longer adequate to encapsulate the academia within which we are operating. All writing traditions evolve over time; perhaps those within our own fields are doing so in a way which would free us up more? Or perhaps there are developments in other areas which could be transplanted and subsequently flourish in our own sphere? Doing things as they have always been done may be closing us down, whereas searching out the new approaches has the potential for opening us up again.

ACADEMIC WRITING: NEW APPROACHES

The 2nd law of thermo dynamics in expressive dance

NOTE

[1] See Chapter 1 and then Chapter 2.

CHAPTER 6

CREATIVE ACADEMIC WRITING

How "Creative" Techniques Can Facilitate Academic Writing

And here we reach a playground furnished with all sorts of magical and fantastical playthings. There is a slide fashioned into a dragon's head, which will take us into another land if we let it. There is the carousel, which could take us flying beyond the skies. There are building bricks in many colours, hula-hoops and juggling balls in red, green, yellow and blue. There is a mirror pool set apart from all activity, carpeted with velvety grass and trailing honeysuckle.

INTRODUCTION

In this chapter I suggest that the blending of certain "creative" writing techniques can facilitate the writing of academic pieces. The techniques are facilitative because they can:

– Encourage us to develop an academic writing voice which we can be comfortable with.
– Encourage writing for discovery.
– Encourage a writing style which flows more smoothly.

The aim of this chapter, then, is to introduce some creative writing techniques which are applicable to academia. These promote our "authentic writing voice", aid enquiry and are tools for an engaging writing manner, thus unblocking us. The sections will look at:

– What are "creative" writing techniques?
– The "authentic writing voice" in academia.
– Writing for discovery.
– Writing blocks.
– Writing strategies.

WHAT ARE "CREATIVE" WRITING TECHNIQUES?

What do I mean by "creative" writing techniques as opposed to any other writing techniques? Writing creatively does not depend on the subject matter. We can write creatively about a computer chip and uncreatively about a sunset over the sea. However, the difference between the two is sometimes difficult to isolate: we just kind of sense it when we encounter it; which isn't very helpful for the apprentice

CHAPTER 6

seeking to develop creative writing techniques. Though, just as with the apprentice, one way we can get a perspective on this is by looking at what others have done before us. We can read. We can read — academic non-fiction, general non-fiction, fiction, poetry — and begin to make comparisons, begin to make choices about what we can appropriate into our own writing because we've found a way of presenting something which appeals to us.

I have introduced various creative writing techniques throughout this book, such as narrative (see Chapter 4) and poetic language (see Chapter 5). Here I want to touch on three more and suggest how they are of interest to academic writers:

– Returning to the joy of writing.
– Word sounds.
– Metaphor.

Returning to the Joy of Writing

The joy of writing? Are you mad? What could be joyful about writing an essay or a thesis or a journal article? The word "joy" attached to "writing" just does not seem to fit with the academic environment. I think this not only an awful pity, but also a loss. A loss to the author and a loss to academia. Academia and research evolve through fresh thinking, innovative perspectives, challenge and the exploration of what was previously the unthinkable. This pioneering potential is often squashed out of work when the writing of it becomes a sort of purgatory. Enjoying the writing process, delighting in the textures and tastes of words and how we can slot them together to form the patterns we call sentences and paragraphs, releases the potential for invention.

When we are writing creatively, we are seriously playing or playing seriously. The oft-repeated quote of CG Jung states: "The creation of something new is not accomplished by the intellect but by the *play instinct* acting from inner necessity." (Quoted in Cameron, 1993, p. 20.) The "play" Jung is advocating puts the player in a relaxed frame of mind, open to new possibilities and making new connections, to allowing the imagination full range. It is a "play" which opens a space for experimentation and discovery. A space which Gilbert and Evans (2000, p. 51) drawing on Winnicot (1971) describe as a "transitional space" allowing for reflection, discussion, exploration and hypothesising. In our own writing practice we can generate this space for ourselves, a safe, playful space, where we are in between what's in our heads and what we have to express to others. Here we have free rein to pull apart, argue with, turn over and examine and poke at material, theories and experiences; our own and others.

> A spirit for play that invites the as-yet-unimagined possibilities in the work to speak has to hover over the field between the researcher and his or her work. Only when the researcher is able to play with the work can the unfinished business of the work find a place in the work. (Romanyshyn, 2007, p. 138.)

Blake gave a less tranquil view of this with his vision of Los, the poetic imagination, forging words from metal and fire. Here we are more aware of the hard work involved, the raging heat, the grimy conditions. Yet there may still be a connection with a notion of play, in that Los is allowing the molten metal to be fashioned by the flames, and it comes to him in a malleable state which he then begins to craft, finding its form as he works.

The point here is that the "play" is with the words — rather than going off for a game of football or for an hour gaming on the computer, though that may help too (see "The Fertile Void" in Chapter 1). We entertain ourselves with the meanings and double meanings of words, with the patterns they make on the page, with the stories and jokes they can tell. And from this pleasing hubbub, new perceptions — the unexpected and previously unthought-of — emerge.

Word Sounds

Words have an aural quality which fascinates; you only have to listen to children learning to speak to hear them playing with the sounds. They also have a rhythm, a beat. Monosyllabic words used in a row can give a strong beat, as opposed to multi-syllabic language tending towards being softer. Certain consonants, like "b", "d", "k", are harder than others such as "s", "m", "sh" and than vowel sounds like "oo" or "aa". In the English language there's a tendency to talk/read giving sentences a di-dum rhythm, an unstressed syllable followed by a stressed one. Repeating word sounds (alliteration) such as "shimmering sands" or "testing tape" gives a sense of flow, a cadence which the ear will pick up on.

As lines on the paper, words also have a visual quality. If we like to doodle, we can notice how the a "w" can become a wave pattern, a "t" the upright and branches of a tree, an "s" the head of a serpent, for instance. We can exaggerate or minimise letters so they take on different shapes and have movement across the page. This is, of course, more difficult to do with words on a computer screen: there is less freedom just to allow the lines to wander and reveal something we had hardly thought of. However, more deliberate manipulation is possible.

We usually talk and write unaware of these aural and visual aspects of language. In fact, we will naturally tend towards using the rhythmic characteristics with barely a second thought. A creative technique is to take more notice of the potential of how words sound and look, then have fun and experiment until we become more discerning of the effects that can be produced.

Along with how the words sound and look, we have meanings. Words that sound the same but have different meanings, such as "sole" and "soul" (homophones). Words that have multiple meanings: for instance, "loaf" as in what we eat and "loaf" as in being idle (homonyms). We can use a thesaurus to find different words which have the same meaning (synonyms) or opposite meanings (antonyms). Again, creative writing, as opposed to any other kind, takes account of this. It uses the full

CHAPTER 6

range of language, it looks for variety in words and is interested in how homophones, homonyms and antonyms can be teasing or open up questions and other possibilities.

> **Example of Playing with Word Sounds**
>
> I wrote this in my writing journal on a morning when I was feeling physically and emotionally under-par.
>
> Stalled.
> Throat swollen.
> No words.
> Stalked.
> Stuck
> in neutral
> with the handbrake on.
> How I want to let
> go, to be free
> wheeling once again —
> splurge, splash into
> words again.
>
> I wrote it very quickly, only adding in "stalked" later on, deliberately echoing the words "stalled" and "stuck". There's the obvious repetition of the "s" sound. The opening monosyllabic words "stalled" and "stuck" have harder consonant sounds than "splurge" and "splash", giving a harsher rhythm and that feeling of being stopped. The repeated "ee" later on gives a more open sound, suggesting the opening up of possibilities.

When we are considering what is "good" writing, we often talk about how it flows. This flow at least partly comes from word choice. We can become more adept at word choice to enhance the smoothness of our academic writing by being more conscious of the aural and visual qualities of words.

Metaphor

Metaphor — the use of a tangible image to explore a more ephemeral experience — is central to writing creatively. It is also, Jaynes (1990, p. 55) suggests, central to how the mind conceives the world: "Subjective conscious mind is an analog of what is called the real world. It is built up with a vocabulary or lexical field whose terms are all metaphors or analogs of behaviour in the physical world."

I am imagining that some of my readers will associate metaphor in writing with the profoundly literary and with a tendency towards obscurity. And, in academia, though metaphor will be used in teaching, it is less acceptable — in some fields — in written pieces. This is unfortunate, for, in line with Jaynes, I believe that we naturally resort to metaphors to explain and find meanings. I have done so many times in this book. Metaphors are concerned with elucidation, opening the blinds and letting the light flood in (oops, there's another one). They are keys to understanding (and another). And indeed, as such they are also central to academic endeavour (Richardson, 2000; Coulehan, 2003; Prendergast, 2004). This is a very brief look at metaphor. If your curiosity is piqued, turn to "Writing Strategies" later in this chapter.

> **Summary Box**
> Re-engaging with the "play" instinct in writing and becoming more adept at our natural instinct to be drawn by word sounds and metaphor, are useful "creative" writing techniques in academia. They have the capacity for encouraging an "authentic writing voice", discovery through writing and a smooth writing style.

THE "AUTHENTIC WRITING VOICE" IN ACADEMIA

What do I mean by "authentic voice" in writing? Why do I think it matters within the academic context? And how will getting to know ours unblock us? At the very basic level, we use our voice to express something about ourselves. Our oral voice has its aural qualities. If this is a face-to-face encounter, there are visual clues to enhance it, furnish its understanding with depth. Our written voice utilises symbols on some kind of surface, symbols which we have communally agreed to recognise as letters. These create words to which we ascribe meaning. Yet these symbols have to work hard in that they develop and establish our "presence on the page", in other words, our writing voice, which is the means by which we express our "aliveness" (Alvarez, 2005, p. 21). Our writing voice is how we communicate something to readers who we are unlikely ever to meet. We are shaking hands with them, looking them in the eyes and saying, "Here, listen to what I have to say." This all happens through the manipulation of some notations which hold no intrinsic meaning in themselves.

Plus, we want to go further. We want our written words to be garnered with import, to carry with them an elucidation of our work, of our knowledge and understandings and of our perspectives; which inevitably means a revelation of our selves. This is where the concept of "authentic" comes in. We want our "presence on the page" to be a genuine and trustworthy representation of what we have discovered, of what we have to say.

An authentic voice also contains the notion that this is a distinctive, an individual, mode of expression. There is a facet to this voice which puts it apart from others. This is what we are striving for in academic writing: an originality, however slight, which adds to our overall picture and understanding of the world around us. To move into metaphor, we are each bringing our piece to the jigsaw to create a more complete whole. Our piece may be blue like the others which are making up the sky;

CHAPTER 6

even so it will be a slightly different shade or shape in order to fit the hole where it will come to link with others.

I am a writer; that's how I think of myself, first and foremost, whatever else I may do, I put words one in front of the other on a page. So I am comfortable with my writing voice. When it came to producing pieces for the academic environment, however, this was new territory. Would I be able to conform enough to have my pieces accepted, while still holding onto enough of my writing voice for it all to sound authentic? For me this particularly meant holding onto the "I" perspective as much as I could, using metaphor and mixing literary references with academic ones.

Feeling at ease with an authentic voice within academia is not always straightforward. In other chapters, we have already seen that some people — perhaps because of ethnicity, educational background, gender or cross-disciplinary working — can feel an "imposter" (see Chapter 2) in their discipline or academia in general. In the last chapter we saw how the conventions of academic writing might mitigate against finding an individual voice. Indeed, the idea that academic writing should have a personality at all or use the first person is controversial within some fields. It is possibly better to talk about a professionally rather than a personally authentic voice, as our writing will be moulded by the customs appropriate to the area we are working in. How much comes through of who we are, when we are outside of our academic role, will depend on our own inclinations and what feels permissible to us. Despite this, an authentic academic writing voice still has significance and is worth attention, given that we want to find a way of representing ourselves and our work on the page which carries with it a validity and a genuineness.

Many times in writing this book I have become confused. Meanings and connections, theories and concepts, my ideas and those from others have all become intertwined. Sometimes they have created a colourful tapestry with a clear and sparkling image; at other times, quite frankly, they have become a dense, knotted muddle. When what we're trying to write about is complex, finding the words and teasing them into sentences which will speak to others is difficult and we can feel very blocked.

Using language creatively is a way of acknowledging that complexity of meaning, of expressing ambivalence and contradictions. Writing creatively can get us through those thorny moments of confusion, expressing the messiness while, to some extent, bringing a form to it which then communicates. Creative writing encourages a richness of language which opens up the author and makes what they are saying alive to the reader (and, since they are the first reader, to themselves). In this way it is an engine which keeps us going, even when what we are trying to enunciate is dense and complicated.

> So what kind of language does this need? It's a kind of practice. We are trying to develop a capacity to enter into that aliveness, and represent that aliveness in ways that won't kill it, even though words cut things up. The re-presentation has to be able to connect to people in a heartfelt way and be complex enough

to awaken not just a logical understanding, but also the sense of it as it lives. When it is living in this way, it is in excess of the words, and more than words can say. So aesthetically, we are learning to differentiate the kind of words that open up its aliveness and the kind of words that close it down. (Galvin & Todres, 2009, p. 309.)

Sometimes words do feel inadequate; they "cut things up", or what we are trying to express appears to go beyond language. That can stop us from writing. However, words are all we have, and the richer they are, the more able they are to sustain depth and complexity. "Creative" writing techniques can lead us to the words which open up rather than close down.

There are moments when we are silenced, when we are groping around to find the words to express what we want to say. On the other hand, our silence might come from being faced by the "unspeakable", the "ineffable" (Van Manen, 1990, p. 114). We want our readers to share our sense of shock or awe, yet the language we have readily available does not seem to do our experience justice. A more creative use of expression is a way through this "epistemological" silence (Van Manen, 1990, p. 114).

Psychologist Romanyshyn (2007, p. 27) suggests that metaphor, in particular, offers the "provisional language" we require in the modern research paradigm. Metaphors are able to carry the liminality, the discursive, the doubt, characteristic of much that is being explored in academia today. In addition, metaphors invigorate our language, make it engaging for ourselves and for our readers. By becoming more open to metaphors and all that they can offer, we can keep ourselves more absorbed in our writing and less likely to dry up.

Summary Box

An authentic academic writing voice which establishes our presence on the page as trustworthy, professional and genuine facilitates writing. How much this writing voice is moulded by conventions, and is different from how we present ourselves elsewhere, will depend on our own personal proclivities and on the discipline we are working within. An authentic academic writing voice using this richness of creative techniques is capable of expressing the complex and the layered, the silences and the doubt, meaning we are less likely to become blocked.

WRITING FOR DISCOVERY

Don't write about what you know, write about what you want to discover. (Faulkner, 2009, p. 59.)

Writing is a remarkable endeavour. We can not only write about our discoveries, but we can also write in order to discover. This is what Torrance et al. (1992) have described as a "think-while-you-write" strategy as opposed to a "think-then-write" one. In developing a creative, open way of writing, we are increasing the potential for a slim idea to become expanded and for a hardly grasped thought to be brought out into the light.

Language bringing forth ideas or ideas bringing forth language: the differing concepts around these propositions have long been tussled over. As Robson (2010, pp. 31–33) notes: "The idea that language guides human thinking and perception has a long and turbulent history." However, he suggests that it is now in the ascendancy, with the weight going behind the proposal that language is "how the human brain focuses on the essential details."

If we accept the merry jig between words and notions, even though we may not be so sure who is taking the lead, then we can conceptualise the activity of writing as providing the perfectly sprung dance floor. Going beyond the ephemeral thought and the spoken word, in that it ties down what we are trying to express, writing "anchors" and "grounds" (Evans, 2011). In doing so, writing gives the opportunity for further exploration, development and discovery. However, in order to capture the ideas which are the most connected to our own authentic voice, we have to ensure that we are not just following the same old patterns of language — matching our feet with the black outlines of steps printed on the floor for the purposes of first teaching the waltz. It is in the practice of writing creatively that we can find a more unguarded and welcoming stance to language forming new ideas or ideas forming new language.

Richardson (2000, p. 923) describes writing as "a method of inquiry". She says, "Writing is validated as a method of knowing." She goes on:

> I write because I want to find something out. I write in order to learn something I didn't know before I wrote it. I was taught, however, as perhaps you were, too, not to write until I know what I wanted to say, until my points were organized and outlined. No surprise, this static writing model coheres with mechanistic scientism and quantitative research. But, I will argue, the model is itself a sociohistorical invention that reifies the static social world imagined by our nineteenth-century foreparents. ... [A]dherence to the model requires writers to silence their own voices and to view themselves as contaminants. (P. 924–925.)

Richardson argues, then, that academia has constructed a way of writing which is "static", which encourages people to think then scribe, which encourages them to keep their voices out as "contaminants". This is, however, only a convention, which adheres to an outmoded view of scientific endeavour. Just as we have moved on in our scientific thinking, so we alter the place writing takes in the research process; thus we move towards writing as part of that process, as part of the method.

The belief that we can only put words down on paper when we have everything straight in our heads can be a huge stumbling block (Phillips & Pugh, 2005; Wellington, 2010). Allowing ourselves to write in a messy, incoherent fashion, acknowledging our doubts in our writing, can be a way of getting started and keeping going. It can also be a way of finding out more about our subject. The creative act of writing, if given some space, will allow the thoughts and ideas which are mere seedlings to take root and begin to flourish (see Chapter 1).

> As I write and write, and read and reread what I have written, the writing speaks to me and reveals meaning. And it is a wonderfully rich and adventurous experience. Writers do not begin with a clear understanding of what they will write. Instead they discover meaning during the frequently chaotic process of writing. The writing process is a journey in mystery, a meaning-making venture. Writers do not begin with a mentally constructed text that needs to be transcribed. Writers engage in an ongoing dialogue with their written words. Out of that dialogue meaning is produced and constructed and revealed. (Leggo, 2008, p. 217.)

We are touching here on different genres of knowledge, and one in particular: the possibility that there is a knowing which we already possess and yet is less immediately available as thought. In academia we quite rightly have to be very conscious of what is going on elsewhere in our subject area, what people are writing or saying and how they are conceptualising. However, this can mean that our deeply held and more intuitive knowledge becomes repressed or snuffed out. Writing creatively can bring us back in touch with this understanding, and, in doing so, can facilitate the flow of our essays or articles or book chapters.

Embodied Language, Embodied Knowing

Knowledge comes from reading, from listening to others, from carrying out experiments, interviews and so on. It can also come from within us, from our thoughts, our puzzlings-out and from our bodies. This has been conceptualised as "embodied" knowing (Galvin & Todres, 2009; Finlay, 2011). Our bodies and our minds are working in concert to fully engage with our research field.

> The body knows
> delicate murmuring
> sensing of some gentle form
> and then it goes.
> *Unformed yet felt...*
> (Galvin & Todres, 2009, p. 313.)

Creative writing techniques allow us to wallow in sounds, with their beats and alliterations. Word sounds connect our writing to our bodies. "The body likes rhythm!" (Dark, 2009, p. 177). Creative writing techniques also incite us to heighten our awareness of all our physical senses — sight, taste, sound, smell and touch (see Chapter 1 under "Writing Strategies"). Creative writing techniques, then, connect us to our bodies; they impel an "embodied" experience which can keep us writing. For example, a health professional described how she struggled to tell bad news to patients through a bodily sensation, her anxiety filling her and leaving her feeling: "Like an onion peeled/Layer by Layer" (Finlay, 2011, p. 171). This gave her data a richness and impact.

CHAPTER 6

> **Summary Box**
>
> Creative writing techniques encourage us to write to discover new information. They also encourage us to access both body and mind as sources of knowing.

WRITING BLOCKS

Whether we are aware of it or not, as soon as we start putting words on the page we are establishing a "presence on the page" (Alvarez, 2005), a voice. This voice may come easily, it may sit easily with us. On the other hand, it may not:, it may feel inauthentic. Writing "inauthentically" can lead to us feeling blocked. What we are producing on the page becomes so dull and leaden (for us and our readers) that we grind to a halt.

As Furman (2006, p. 561) states, creative forms of expression elicit a "deep" and "powerful" reaction. In doing so, they hold the reader. Since we are our first readers of our work, they hold us too. Boredom may be a signal of some emotional upheaval we are unwilling to face (see Chapter 2) or it may be a result of our writing being, well, frankly tedious. This is a real turn-off both to us and to any of our readers. It will stop us from writing. It will stop our readers from their continued perusal and from encouraging us to go on.

We may also become blocked because we run out of things to say. We do not have the capacity to plumb the depths of our material so our store of ideas runs dry. Without Leggo's "dialogue" described above (Leggo, 2008), between the tied-down written word and ephemeral thinking, we are likely to find it more difficult to keep going as our knowing becomes dammed up. Writing freely, creatively, chaotically allows the dam to release its load.

In this chapter I have introduced the idea of "embodied" knowing. Not having access to our embodied knowing may block us because we risk being half-informed about our material (see also "parallel process" in Chapter 3). However, mind and body working in concert can unblock us in another way. Writing that comes from the head alone can sometimes lead to rumination, thoughts turning round and round and in on themselves, not coming to any conclusion. This might elicit critical thoughts about ourselves: "I'm not good enough", "I'll never get this done". Connection with the body brings us out of our heads and into our whole selves, which can assist in breaking that cycle of destructive cogitation.

> **Summary Box**
>
> Writing blocks may occur because we are not able to develop an authentic "presence on the page" which we feel easy with or because we run dry of ideas or because we eschew the potential of "embodied" knowing.

WRITING STRATEGIES

Creative writing techniques — including becoming more aware of word sounds and rhythms and more adept at fashioning metaphor (see below) — can reawaken in us the joy of writing. They can help us to develop our own authentic academic writing voice and they encourage writing for discovery. They help our writing to flow, holding the attention of our readers and ourselves.

One way of reacquainting ourselves with creative writing techniques is through keeping a "writing journal", as described in Chapter 1. This is a place where we write regularly, for ourselves, and without concern for rules or conventions. A place where we can just get raw thoughts and notes down. This needn't take a lot of time: fifteen minutes each day is ample for getting started with the regular writing practice. And having your writing journal (whether it be digital or paper-based) near at hand during the day means you can scribble down things as they occur to you. They are there for you to go back to and work with when you have more time..

Another strategy is to utilise a thesaurus regularly. Oxfordictionaries.com suggests that there are, at the very least, a quarter of a million distinct English words. That is an awful lot of choice for us writers. A relatively straightforward way of enriching our language is to use a good thesaurus. I have one open now in my version of Word on the computer. It is perfectly adequate, acceptable satisfactory. It is sufficient, ample, enough for my purposes.

This may be enough to get us through our present blocks. On the other hand, we may want to explore (in our fifteen minutes a day) creative writing techniques in more detail. There are tips on this throughout this book and workshops and courses abound. Here I want to focus on just one technique which bears a great deal more exploration: metaphor.

Metaphor

A metaphor explores something by comparing it with something else. It is a comparison that seeks to "heighten the object of comparison" (Dobyns, 2003, p. 12). In other words, it aims to help us to understand *more* about whatever it is we are trying to investigate. Psychologist Jaynes (1990) suggests that metaphor chimes closely with the way the brain works, in that it is always looking for comparisons with what it already knows, to understand what's new.

Metaphor litters the English language: whoops, there's another one. What meaning do we ascribe to the word "litter"? That there's a lot of it, perhaps? That it's everyday? That it's detritus? That it's thrown away carelessly? Apart from when it becomes a cliché, I would not want metaphor linked with rubbish, but the rest works for me. However, I could have chosen to say that metaphor splatters the English language, or metaphor infiltrates the English language. And I would have loaded the word "metaphor" with slightly different meaning.

CHAPTER 6

Metaphors are also individual, as we will all have our own spin on a word. Until I wrote the paragraph above, I had not thought of the litter-detritus link affecting how metaphor might be understood. However, for others the first implication of "litter" is of debris and waste.

Finally, metaphors are exciting for our purposes because they are layered, they can be explored using all the senses. For example, "My relationship is like a rose garden," is a somewhat clichéd image. However, let's unpack it. What words do we associate with roses? Sweet-scented? Richly coloured? Prickly? What state is the garden in? Well tended? Overly manicured? Weedy? Have the plants become old and ragged? So we can see, that by being more descriptive we can "heighten" the meaning, we can go below the surface.

An exercise in metaphor Today, at this moment, you are a piece of furniture. Describe yourself in great detail. Remember to use all the different senses. What state of repair are you in? What can you be used for? What can't you be used for? What are you used for? What do you resent being used for? Where are you habitually placed? Where would you like to be placed?

Other useful starting points for metaphors are: fruit; weather; journeys; animals (real or imagined); landscapes. Always engage the different physical senses when describing something metaphorically. Useful questions are along the lines of: What state is it in? What would nourish it or help it to flourish? What state would it like to be in?

Metaphor and academic writing Metaphors tend to percolate into all human communications, so they will almost inevitably seep into academic writing. By being more consciously aware of this we have the potential to increase our understanding of aspects of our academic work and research. Metaphor is also valuable in exploring ourselves as writers and what might be getting in the way of our writing (see "Writing Strategies" in Chapter 2). Here, however, I want to focus on how we can use metaphor to enhance our communication with others.

Choose a piece of your own writing: perhaps some notes for an essay or some research notes or a draft of an extract of your thesis or of an article you're working on. Read it and identify any metaphors you are already using. Pick one of the metaphors and write about it descriptively, using all the senses (as with the exercise above).

On the other hand, you can start from the other end, thinking about an aspect of what you are trying to explore or express and seeing if an image appears, or asking yourself, if this were a fruit what fruit would it be? if this were a landscape what landscape would it be? if this were weather, what would it be? Go on until you have a few answers written down and you can choose one which sparks your interest the most. Once again, the idea is to leave the initial stimulus behind and go with the metaphor, describing it, "unpeeling it", turning it over and over until you've depicted it from all angles.

I have used metaphor throughout this book. I wanted to use it to aid understanding and also to demonstrate how it can enrich a text as well as being a jumping-off point for the reader to take the ideas presented and make them applicable to their own situation. Metaphors are a great way of engaging the reader, allowing them into the conversation with the author. For instance, the swampy "hazardous ground" image came to me as I was writing notes for the chapter on the myriad emotional roots for writing blocks. I also had a picture of a rather porky, benign dragon smoking, which I sketched in my writing journal and included in the text. When I sent this chapter out for feedback, it was obvious that this suggestion that the dragons (writing blocks) may not be as ferocious as we think they are had caught the imagination of my readers.

CONCLUSION: A NEW GENRE — CREATIVE ACADEMIC WRITING

In some ways I am suggesting a new genre of writing: creative academic writing. This does, of course, owe much to another genre, creative non-fiction, fact-based writing which employs techniques such as word sounds and rhythm, metaphor and narrative (see Chapter 4) to connect with the reader. Using creative writing skills such as these (and they are described throughout this book) offers the potential for discovery and for presenting the depth of our work. They can also assist in the development of our authentic academic writing voice; a voice which is powerful and engaging both for us and for our audiences.

Fortuitously, creative writing techniques rely on a heightened awareness of capabilities we have very often been using since childhood: specifically, a playfulness with sound and beat and with metaphor. Once we are more attentive to how we (and others) already use word sounds and metaphor, we can be more deliberate about it, enriching and progressing our writing. A mild peppering of creative techniques within our essays, theses or articles, then, can help us through writing blocks. They can also assist us in finding the modes of expression which do justice to our insight and our material.

CHAPTER 7

CASE STUDIES

Experiences of Writing Blocks Within the Academic Environment

INTRODUCTION

As part of my research for this book I have conducted four interviews and present them here as case studies. For these case studies I have used a phenomenological approach, drawing on Spinelli's (1989, p. 29) definition:

> At its most basic level, phenomenology presents itself as a science of experience. Experience from a phenomenological perspective includes within it all mental phenomena, such as wishes, memories, precepts, hypotheses, theories, etc. By employing a specific approach — the phenomenological method — phenomenologists attempt to arrive at increasingly adequate (though never complete or final) conclusions concerning our experiences of the world.

In these case studies I am hoping to bring myself and my readers closer to the experience of writing blocks in their many different hues. I am offering an invitation to delve into their many layers. I am drawing on an interpretative phenomenology where "the researcher's interpretations are understood to be inextricably intertwined with the research findings and the researcher-participant (inter-)subjectivity is embraced" (Finlay, 2011, p. 109). I acknowledge my presence in that I was interviewer and what came out in each interchange was somehow co-created by me and my interviewee (Finlay & Evans, 2009, p. 21)

I was then selector and interpreter of what I have chosen to present here. In this book, I encourage writing as a means of discovery. This is very much a part of my practice. When I write, I research; when I research, I write: the two inexorably feed into each other. In the writing-up of these case studies, in the dance of words which creates this exposition of another's experience, my hand has been on the conductor's baton. I, therefore, work reflexively, with self-awareness of my part in the construction of the stories which are told here. I insert the "I" of me, the author, explicitly into the text. And in this my aim has been for an authenticity, a touching of a kernel of genuineness, rather than for some grand claims of truth. As van Manen (1990, p. 31) says: "A phenomenological description is always one interpretation, and no single interpretation of human experience will ever exhaust the possibility of yet another complementary, or even potentially richer or deeper description."

I have two main reasons for including case studies. Firstly, we all have our own personal and individual experiences of writing blocks. We can become overwhelmed by the sense that this is only happening to us, that only *we* ever feel this way. Perhaps on reading other people's stories you will find resonances and realise that the difficulties created by writing blocks are more universal than you at first thought. Or perhaps you are in a supportive role and are finding it difficult to unravel the writing block which is blighting the work of the person you are helping. Again, maybe finding echoes in the case studies here will help with understanding and finding a way forward. Secondly, the interviews were a rich source of material for this book. I had few expectations of what I would ascertain through my co-researchers'[1] narratives. However, what I have discovered has both informed and illustrated the other chapters in this book.

Ethics

No formal ethical approval was sought for these case studies, however I did reflect and take advice on the ethical dimension. I worked within the structure of informed and "process" consent (Finlay & Molano-Fisher, 2008, p. 257). Interviewees were given the opportunity to read their interview transcripts and to bracket out material if they so desired. I also secured for myself ongoing and adequate supervision and guidance.

Method

Data collection in each case comprised one in-depth, unstructured interview which lasted an hour. I based each interview around the question: "What is your experience of writing blocks?" Other questions were asked during the interview to either clarify or expand on my co-researcher's narrative. I transcribed the interview and sent it to my co-researcher, so that they could bracket out material if they wished. I then "dwelt" with the transcript, allowing the story and the themes to present themselves (Finlay, 2011, p. 98). I began to write and in the writing discovered further layers and complexities. What appears on the following pages is a result of an iterative writing-reading-dwelling-rewriting process.

CASE STUDY 1: THE LONELINESS OF A LONG-DISTANCE WRITER

Mark Turner[2] is a mature student returning to higher education after a break of a number of years to do a postgraduate masters-level qualification. As I read and re-read the transcript of his interview and allowed his words to percolate, three core experiences and meanings began to take shape:

– The lone warrior.
– "Right back into the here and now".
– A singular journey.

Themes

The lone warrior At the beginning of the interview, there is a strong, almost abrasive energy. Mark characterises his writing block as a means for getting what he wants, and what he wants is: to gain a sense of control over what is happening to him in the educational environment; and to be noticed.

He explains how he would feel unable to write and then miss the deadlines set for his assignments. Yet the way he describes what happens suggests something active rather than passive. His writing block is a weapon for "blowing" or "busting" the deadlines.

> I'm setting the agenda; once that deadline's gone, I'm setting the agenda. Not someone else. That's a big thing. I'm setting the agenda, not you.

He acknowledges the "adversarial" aspects of this, the sense of him being in some kind of struggle with those who set and assess his work. He says he wants his learning to be about personal development and growth. He sees his tutors as setting up academic "hoops" and "hurdles" to be negotiated and believes that these get in the way of his own goals. The pay-off for this stance is that he often loses marks. This is less important to him than maintaining control.

> What actually mattered from the start to the finish is what I got out of my learning process, not what marks someone gave it; that was irrelevant. Apart from, you know there's a difference between a pass and a fail, obviously, as long as I got a pass I didn't see that it mattered.

The second thing Mark wants is to be noticed, to stand out. And by not writing, by being blocked, and missing deadlines, he stands out.

> Perhaps it's about standing out and being different. In order to bring out my work, it has to be some how, shape or form different from other people's and blowing the deadline is the only way, or one way, I've learnt to stand out.

His desire to stand out, however, staunches his writing process in another way. He doesn't believe that the self he wants to be noticed can appear in academic writing.

> I lose something in bringing it back out and putting it down in a form that's completely incoherent to me. Somebody else has already written a better book than I could produce and I've already devoured however many of those, so just rehashing it and putting it on paper is, to me, a real waste of time.

The academic writing form is alien, it is constraining, it is "incoherent", it is merely "rehashing". It is "unrelated" to what he needs to know. What appears to be underlying this for Mark is that he is not finding his own voice in academic writing; he does not find himself and his own unique perspective in it. His writing is blocked

CHAPTER 7

because he feels that whenever he tries to write he won't be noticed, he won't stand out, in the words he puts down.

One representation of Mark's writing block is as a weapon. It is a method for him to regain control, a foil with which to fence off the "them" who "have power" over him. It is part of his armoury. By missing deadlines he will be noticed and if he writes he will not, because his voice, his way of seeing things, will not appear in the "rehashing" of other people's words required by academia. Being different, standing out and setting his own agenda are key conditions for Mark; and his writing block, at first sight, appears as a weapon to realise these principles.

"Right back into the here and now" However, as the interview progresses, the energy turns from combative to more introspective, and the steel plating takes on a defensive, shielding role. The writing block acquires a different character:

> If I get too immersed in a subject and suddenly I don't know who I am in that anymore, then I leave it well alone. Because of the subject matter, it might push all my buttons, then I'm like floating off, just losing it, losing my sense of myself. ... And I have to leave it, find myself again and then go round the other business, things I have to do, until I've got enough courage to go back into whatever it was that I lost me in, try again.

The subject matter itself becomes the trigger for the block as it brings painful emotions and difficult, uncomfortable thoughts "right back into the here and now". Mark becomes immersed in what he is researching and writing and is unable to maintain a distance; everything becomes "here and now", as troubling, as raw, as disturbing as if he is the experiencer rather than the witness. Mark's writing block is then a way of protecting himself from this disturbing swirl of emotions. Not writing means that he doesn't have to feel like he's "losing it".

He experiences writing as an intensely solitary activity, so when he is writing about material which distresses him, he feels alone with that distress, which he knows is not healthy for him.

> Part of my resistance to writing when I get a bit weird is this self-respect, is my respect for myself. And my sanity, and what I'm learning is ... that doing things in isolation doesn't help. ... Writing by nature is a solitary occupation. Maybe, back in my other degree, having people around me in the halls of residence, I knew I wasn't alone. Some of the issues were a bit close to home, but I had people around me, you know, it was a very close community; whereas I don't have that now.

In addition, Mark has a strong sense of there being certain writing which is "useful", and "navel gazing" writing which is not. He describes the latter as "self-indulgent nonsense". He is avoiding a particular way of writing, partly because of the emotional intensity of it and partly because he categorises it as not being constructive.

Another view of Mark's writing block is that it is defensive rather than offensive. It is protecting him from material which raises distressing and difficult emotions. He feels alone in his writing and so needs to guard himself against what it might bring up for him. He might do this by stopping his flow or by denigrating a certain type of writing as "nonsense", and, therefore, without function.

A singular journey   As already noted, Mark feels alone in his writing. No-one else can understand what he goes through to put the words on the paper; no-one else grasps the significance of what he is articulating. He writes alone; he feels no connection with the writing process or with his eventual audience (his assessing tutors). He feels unsupported. He feels solitary. And this makes it hard to keep going.

> The journey that I'm on is a singular journey, geographically, mentally, spiritually. Who else understands what I'm writing about? Not many.

This lack of a sense of audience stops him writing in another way too. It makes his efforts appear futile, as he is speaking but there is no-one to hear.

> I don't know where's the place to exhibit written work? I could go and graffiti it on a subway somewhere. ... [With an] essay, whatever I say will get read by one person and then it will go into an archive. That's it. So actually, unless I get something personal out of it in terms of my growth and my learning, it's a waste of time. Maybe that's a bit harsh. It feels harsh. And maybe it is harsh. That's how it is.

Without companions on his personal and educational journey, or listeners for his words, Mark feels isolated and putting effort into his writing feels futile. This saps his motivation to keep going, which blocks his work.

Discussion

The themes presented by Mark's transcript lead me to the following concepts which I want to explore further:

– Combative and protective writing blocks.
– Writing blocks are layered.
– Feeling alone in writing may lead to blocking.

In the short story *The Loneliness of the Long Distance Runner* by Alan Sillitoe, Colin Smith stops just before the finishing line of the race he could easily win and lets the other runners pass him by. He does so to have his revenge for the brutal treatment he has received at the hands of the borstal staff where he has been incarcerated. His winning would have been a good publicity coup for them. Colin Smith wielded the only power he had. By doing so he forfeited his own personal triumph.

When I was reading the transcript of the interview with Mark, Sillitoe's story came to mind. The parallel I immediately made was that Mark also stops before the finishing line of a race he could complete. He also feels it is the only power he has and he recognises the adversarial element in what he is doing. In addition, he also pays a forfeit in losing marks. There were two other elements to the story which seemed to echo through the transcript. Firstly, Colin Smith, a vulnerable young man, has to devise ways of safeguarding himself in a harsh regime where he finds he has no voice. Secondly, he chooses the loneliness of long-distance running, he chooses to be alone, both as a means of protection and as a way of giving himself the space to be himself and think.

Of course, it would be facetious of me to suggest that academia has any similarities with Sillitoe's cruel borstal regime. However, Mark obviously holds on to a strong "me against them" dynamic. It is possible that this is how he usually approaches life in general or education in particular. It may also be connected with previous learning experiences. On the other hand, the academic structure can encourage an adversarial attitude. Any configuration where there is one set of people evaluating another tends to cast those judging as "them" who "have power" and those who are being judged as being without control. How much this is entrenched and perpetuated will depend on the institution, the assessors and also the assessed. The leeway or backing given to tutors and/or students who are willing to collaborate on and discuss marking and assessment will vary. The appearance of how evaluation is conducted, though, can strengthen a student's own belief in their place in the power hierarchy, and, as with Mark, a writing block may be a tool for regaining some control.

Mark's concern with setting his own agenda and wanting to be noticed do not appear to be confined to the educational setting. They are guiding principles for him. And they bring him into conflict with how he experiences academic writing to be. The only way he can be noticed is by stopping writing. If he continues writing, then he disappears in an "alien" world of rehashed words. Again, are the conditions for this belief partly created by academia? Do the conventions of academic writing, or the way they are presented to the student, reinforce this sense of having no personal voice and of being asked merely to regurgitate what others have said?[3] The idea that I have no voice and anything I say will just be lost in a morass may well lead to feelings of futility until the writing eventually grinds to a halt. The paradox is that if Mark did hand in his work then he might get noticed for bringing something worthwhile to the debate. Is this also a fear? That he will make an impact with his writing, rather than that he won't?

However, Mark's writing blocks are not only adversarial, they are also protective. They protect him from feeling what he senses he cannot deal with. They encourage him to take a look and then move back out of harm's way. He is defending his vulnerabilities, the tender spots, the nerve endings which interlace and connect like a spun spider's thread with his subject matter. His writing blocks are a way of keeping him safe. There may be other ways, though, for him to deal with the emotional impact, and the writing itself could be one answer. Using certain techniques in writing can offer the possibility for keeping going while maintaining a distance from the material. This fine judgement between being connected, while at the same time holding an outside perspective, with our subject matter is not an easy one to maintain and takes some practice[4]. On the other hand, it is a strategy which has the potential to address a writing block which aims to safeguard the author.

Colin Smith chooses the loneliness of long-distance running because it gives him time to think and gets him out of the oppressive environment of the borstal. Mark has not consciously chosen to be solitary in his writing: he thinks that this is how it has to be, how it inevitably is. He has no sense of writing being relational, or that it could be a supported, collaborative activity[5]. Each time he sets out on a writing journey, he is resigned to setting out alone. This can set him on the road to feeling blocked, partly because when things get tough, there is no-one to turn to, and partly because he doesn't have the sense that his writing will be received and listened to, that it will make a difference, that he will be noticed.

Unpeeling Mark's writing blocks with him demonstrates the many layers which often underlie an individual's inability to keep going. Adversarial or dismissive language can be a protective screen for something else. Expressions of boredom or "It's a waste of time" may be easier to say than "This is emotionally charged" or "challenging". They are often easier to say because academic writing is not supposed to be about feelings, which may mean that the emotional aspects of writing blocks are more frequently overlooked[6].

Summary box

Writing blocks can be combative and protective.
Writing blocks are layered.
Aloneness in writing can block.

CASE STUDY 2: DARING TO

Sue[7] is an academic who teaches and supervises at graduate and postgraduate levels. She has begun a PhD but not completed one. In contrast to Mark's, her story is not a solitary one; indeed, it is a copiously peopled one. The core concepts which present themselves to me are:

– Ghosts and cheerleaders.
– "The beast".
– How dare I? ↔ I dare.
– Written into the body.

Themes

Ghosts and cheerleaders   Sue's narrative is peopled with characters — real and imagined, present and absent, from her past and from her now. Her experience of writing and writing blocks is not a solitary one but, on the contrary, a highly relational one.

CHAPTER 7

There are the "ghosts" from her personal history, whose words are hardly acknowledged as being separate from her own because they feel so familiar. The idea of doing further qualifications would elicit:

Don't get too big for your boots. Dr Sue? What're you thinking of?

She has inherited the sense that further education and higher qualifications are for others. They don't fit her, somehow: they are too grand, they are not for her. She has to stay in her place, a modest, unassuming place.

Then there are the present-day spectres: real and fantasised reactions from colleagues known and unknown to her:

It was a fear, you know, an anxiety about putting it down and then somebody saying, well that's rubbish. ... We're quite good about gunning [others] down and going phut, get you. Chopping them down.

In Sue's experience, there is something noxious at the centre of academia which creates a context where ghouls can thrive. She calls it the "stuff" of the academic world, such as the "construct" whereby "they think, well, if the university has got more staff with doctorates, then they're a better university, and you go, 'No, not necessarily.'"

If you're looking at what can stop you writing, particularly in an academic context, it's (a) your audience and (b) people who might also be there either willing you to do it or in either very tacit or implicit ways inhibiting you. I've seen good supervision but I've also experienced very, very bad supervision, when you think, what are you scared of? And again, they're under pressure, from the academy and from other things. But none of that is ever explicitly stated, it feels, you know that's all implicit and has not to be exposed, because, again, that's about vulnerability isn't it?

What Sue was looking for in her own writing journey were "pom-poms and cheerleading". She wants somebody to say, "Yeah, it's OK to do this, yes it's scary, it's exposing, but, you know, go get the bloody thing written." Instead, what she remembers most are the "ghosts" from her past and less ethereal beings who had their own reasons — some benign, some less so — for not wanting to support or encourage her forward.

"The beast" In Sue's narrative, her PhD, and PhDs in general, are living things, with minds of their own. She describes watching a colleague print out her final thesis and calls it "the beast". "It was like a bit of herself [being churned out] ... I don't think I could have ever lived with that kind of beast in my house." The beast is malevolent, it is "a very toxic thing". It "destroys people". And "that destructive process isn't about the research, it's about writing it up." In the writing process, the thoughtful ideals which were the impetus for starting the research become poisoned; and the final written piece, the "it", is morphed into a creature which is both terrifying and all-consuming.

> The people who do come out the other end with PhDs are, have to be, very, very selfish, very, very unrelational with the people they work with, completely single-minded, completely focused and, you know, piss everybody off to get there. ... [A] PhD, it occupies your entire sense of being.

For Sue, the "beast" requires "sacrifice" — too much, in her opinion. "I couldn't have it take over my life ... I couldn't see it being important enough to find the time and the energy to find time to write."

In Sue's story, the task of writing up a PhD became so mammoth, the "sacrifices" demanded by the "beast" so huge, that she walked away from it.

How dare I? ↔ I dare   The rhetorical question, "How dare I?" recurs during the interview in different guises. Firstly, there is a daring in the analysis of the interview data: "How dare you make those interpretations of somebody else's words?" This caution comes from a sense of respect and of wanting to do the best by her interviewees, who had shared their stories with her.

Beyond that, there is the daring required to bring her perspective into the academic world. There is the sense of "exposure", the feeling that in theorising or making statements in any way, she is acting somehow above her competence, being "grandiose". "It assumed a huge magnitude of import ... how dare I do that? That seemed a big thing for me to carry on my shoulders ... a grandiose statement to make."

Sue struggled with her desire to effect change through her research and her words, set against the concerns encompassed by the words, "How dare I?" The writing block became more entrenched when she was faced with the possibility that all her work would not alter anything for those she had interviewed and the many like them, and when she began to wonder how much difference having a PhD would make to her personally.

> I was very, very clear about why I wanted to do it and it was about making changes and being on a mission, and wanting to improve people's experiences. ... Once I couldn't do that, it became a bit impotent, I guess; well what's the bloody point of this? ... Who would you write it for? What's the point? ... What difference would I have been able to make anyway? And how much of a difference will it make to your own sense of self, actually having it?

It has taken many years, but Sue has come to a point where she now does dare.

> So all that stuff, you can't do that, just went. Maybe you can, other people do, why can't you? You know, be brave about it, 'cos all you're saying is this is your interpretation of what happened in that particular event; what's wrong with that? Make those claims, 'cos they're only your claims. That's quite liberating, actually.

CHAPTER 7

Her energy for writing, for giving voice to those interviewed, for "giving voice to the voiceless", has come back. But it comes with the realisation that:

> It's just not going to be that thesis. It couldn't be in a thing that was four inches thick and read by three people. It had to be accessible to others.

When Sue hit a wall with her PhD, she went to some creative writing classes. She explains, "That's really when everything changed for me because I could write. It was only an hour workshop but I, you know, wrote. And from that experience I ended up writing poems from my data." These poems were not well received by her PhD supervisor; however, they did end up on a professional website.

> The poetry that came out of the PhD is now on the Queen's Nursing Institute website for anybody to possibly come across, and I didn't ever stop myself thinking that was a bloody good idea. When the woman who runs the Queen's Nursing Institute said do it, I went, OK, I will. And I did. And they are not my best poems because they're the first poems that I wrote, and I wrote them six years ago, but I never once thought, Don't do it, because it gives a voice to those people who I interviewed.

Sue has made the journey from the paralysing, "How dare I?" to the more liberating, "I dare". This has been made possible, at least partly, by her coming to realise that: her interpretation is just that, hers, one amongst many. She is also investigating other ways, apart from a PhD, for staying true to her "mission" of effecting change through "giving voice to the voiceless". This has loosened up once again her writing hand.

Written into the body Sue portrays what happened in her body when she experiences her writing block. She describes the "feeling tired, lassitude, deeply depressed, really horrible energy drain" which comes over her as she sits at the computer unable to write. These physical feelings bludgeoned her, affected her markedly, not only stopping her from writing, but also leading to serious illness.

Those symptoms return to her even now when she faces particularly challenging academic writing projects: "The whole physical response is so learned that I've got to unlearn it. ... It's just like, oh, I've been doing that for ten years, you know, so trying to get past that."

The writing block has become so ingrained as to initiate a physical response to sitting in front of a computer. All the anxiety, fear and demotivation which were churned up by her PhD have now been translated into bodily symptoms. Yet they return when the writing is not about the PhD; they have been transposed onto other writing experiences. Phobic responses can be characterised as when a response appropriate in one situation goes into overdrive and becomes attached to other less threatening experiences. For instance, the fear induced during a car crash spills over into any car journey. Sue's experience of her writing block has a phobic parallel, in that the feelings in her body are reproduced even in writing environments unconnected with her PhD.

Discussion

The themes presented by Sue's transcript lead me to the following concepts which I want to explore further:

– Writing is relational; writing is to or for someone.
– Writing blocks have meaning.

Sue's narrative shows a journey, a journey which is filled with people, with relationships[8]. Real and imagined, past and present, there are the "ghosts" which attempt to hold her back and put her down and the "cheerleaders" which spur her onwards. Around the time of tackling her PhD (which also has a personality of its own: "the beast") the "ghosts" appear to have had the upper hand. Both the ancient "ghosts" with their "You're not up to this", which she had inherited, and the more present day "ghosts" which she attributes to a tendency in academia to "chop" and "gun" others down. The "ghosts" reinforced the "How dare I?" concern, whereas the cheerleaders would push her towards the "I dare" stance.

Sue experiences her writing block in a very physical way. I made a connection with the symptoms of the people she was interviewing. Sue agreed it was a possibility though did not seem to credit it with a lot of credence; and fatigue, lassitude and lack of energy are indicators of a myriad of conditions. Yet I am drawn back to that first thought I had as I reread the transcript and type up this case study. Could there be a link between the way Sue's writing block manifested itself and the illness she was exploring?

Or perhaps there is another echo to be found. Sue's impetus for doing her research was to give voice to people who, she was discovering, were often not listened to intently enough; in her parlance they were "voiceless". In the course of her work, she became "voiceless" too. Her writing block was giving her an understanding of what it was like to be without voice; thus, perhaps, bringing her closer to what her interviewees were expressing.

Sue describes her writing block as an "embodied experience", since she feels it in her body. Embodiment can also mean the body and mind working in concert to create understanding and knowledge. It's also possible to see her writing block in this light, as giving her some further information about her research participants' symptoms and experience of being "voiceless".[9]

On the other hand, it could also have been offering insight into her own personal motivations and direction[10]. Sue's writing block heralded a turning point in her life. Though incredibly painful and debilitating at the time, it has led her to explore writing in more innovative and engaging ways. It is no longer a torture to write. She is beginning to find a clearer, more authentic writing voice within academia and elsewhere. She has moved from "How dare I?" to "I dare.

It's not easy to pay attention to a writing block. It is a challenging, distressing, frustrating and awkward thing which elicits all sorts of critical judgements about ourselves and our environments. However, it is possible that a writing block does have something to say either about our research material or about our own goals and

CHAPTER 7

how to attain them. Sometimes it is easier to shoulder the burden of a writing block if we believe we can discover something new from it.

> **Summary box**
> Writing is relational; writing is to or for someone.
> Writing blocks have meaning.

CASE STUDY 3: FINDING A PLACE TO START

After a period of time working, Sarah[11] has returned to university to embark on a PhD. Her research is cross-disciplinary and, though she has been a resident in the UK for a long time, English is her second language. As I spent time with the transcript of my interview with her, three themes began to present themselves:

– "It's walls in my head."
– Finding what's missing.
– Academic self.

Themes

"It's walls in my head"   Sarah has successfully completed a draft of her first PhD chapter, a literature review. She is now struggling with subsequent chapters and with writing an article she wants to submit to a journal. She describes procrastinating, finding other things to do rather than writing. When she does begin writing, she invariably doesn't finish. What underlies this pattern of behaviour are feelings: a lack of confidence; a "fear of failure"; a "fear of not finishing". These are what she calls the "walls in my head".

> I procrastinate. ... I write all sorts of outlines and then lack the confidence to take them further. ... I end up procrastinating and doing other things.

The words "lack of confidence" come up several times during the interview. She links it to the fear of getting it wrong and of not finishing.

> I can get quite panicky about it ... I end up feeling I really haven't got a clue what I'm doing; that I'm going about it all the wrong way; and I'm just not going to finish it. I find it very hard to think clearly then, when I feel like that, which makes it even harder to write anything. I just leave it for a bit and I start again with a different idea and in the end I've got lots of unfinished lists, outlines of things and never really get anywhere with it.

But it isn't just about not getting it wrong, and the pressure is about more than getting it right: it is about getting it perfect, even the first draft. This becomes further exacerbated when she is preparing to show her work to an audience, such as her supervisors, or when thinking about writing for journal submission.

> [When I'm] writing for an audience, I'm more aware of the fear, I mean the pressure of having to get it just right.

The "wanting to do it perfectly", and being anxious that she isn't, leads to "thinking I'm not good enough to do it". The cycle is perpetuated: lack of confidence leads to her writing block, which stops her from producing. She then has no evidence to counter her fear of not being good enough and of not being able to finish. She is aware of this dynamic and is trying to address it:

> That can be one sort of hurdle as well, got to be perfect on the first draft, rather than just a draft. [However] I am getting better at that, just getting ideas, a few ideas, down.

Meanwhile her writing block still manifests itself as a lot of deferring action. The thought of writing this particular article is "such a dull cloud I just try to push it to one side, which is not really helpful, I suppose".

Sarah identifies the emotional basis — "the walls in my head" — for her writing block, which reveals itself in procrastination. The one feeds into the other, as lack of a finished article undermines further her confidence in being able to finish.

Missing Sarah describes becoming overwhelmed with options and not knowing how to find a focus for her article.

> [There's] just too many ideas in there [my head], and floating about and [it's difficult] trying to cram everything into one article.

And there's a fear being elicited here too: the fear that in whittling down, she might miss out what's most important. The word "missing" is repeated in the interview. When asked to reflect on this, Sarah offers:

> I worry about losing something, missing something or forgetting about something, it feels quite chaotic at times. I think this is a reflection of my surroundings being quite chaotic. ... I've got stuff all over the place and it just feels like a big mess and it feels a bit like that in my head sometimes. And yes, always missing things and looking for things and I can't find that book or that paper and I think that would make a big difference having it all in one place: tidier, physical surroundings but also in my head. There is the space there, it's just a block to tidying it up and clearing it up. A bit like the writing. So there's definitely a parallel there, I'd agree with that; internal and external chaos.

Sarah could find the physical space in her environment which would be less chaotic, only she does not. She has found one way of being less concerned about "missing" something in her writing:

> Every day I was writing a diary and writing down what's on my mind, even just writing how difficult it is. I found that really useful ... I know I can get back to it because sometimes I feel there's too much in there [my head] almost,

> and writing it down means it's there to go back to. ... I think through writing. It helps me to think through something and make sense of it. It's not just writing to get the ideas out but it can help to generate new ideas.

However, as with the not creating the physical space, there is something holding her back from keeping on with the diary, even though she finds it useful. When asked what is holding her back, she replies: "Myself", perhaps eluding to the cycle of self-sabotage portrayed above.

On the other hand, maybe there is also an aspect of the academic environment which is not helpful. A creative person in generating ideas and making connections, Sarah feels that some of the constraints of academic writing make it harder for her to be truly expressive. They dampen down that important creative characteristic within herself.

> Yes, I suppose it's having that need to be creative and then having to force it onto that narrow format [of the journal]. Yeah, I suppose it's a mismatch there.

Fearing she might miss out something important; working in a physical environment which makes it harder for her be sure she is not losing something, both in reality and metaphorically; the creative facet being missing from some types of academic writing: all these aspects of the word "missing" undermine Sarah's ability to keep going.

Academic self Sarah sometimes struggles to see herself as a "proper" academic. This is at least partly due to her returning to academia after a break and to her research being cross-disciplinary. However, it also appears to be a more commonly held concern.

> A lot of PhD students talk about feeling an imposter. Just sort-of playing at it.

Who are the "proper" academics? For Sarah, they are her audience, the people who are going to read her article, for instance, and judge it harshly. To be an "imposter" in front of those who have attained the "proper" status, those who have arrived in some sense, is a difficult situation to be in. It adds to the sense of being wrong which Sarah is already carrying with her.

Despite good and supportive supervision, because of personal circumstances Sarah feels more solitary in her writing than she would like.

> It feels lonely sometimes. I quite like working by myself, I'm quite happy just being by myself generally. But I think it would be helpful at times to have more contact.

Time, other commitments and geographical considerations mean it is difficult for Sarah to be as integrated into an academic writing community as she would find desirable. Being alone can make being motivated or working through the rockier times harder, meaning that blocks could be more likely to occur.

Discussion

Extrapolating from Sarah's transcript I have identified these ideas for further exploration:

– Writing blocks are not necessarily about inactivity.
– The words used to describe a writing block can lead to a greater understanding of it.
– Writing blocks can be iterative and dynamic.

Sarah keeps busy, doing things that it is necessary for her to do. She does lists and outlines. Her writing block does not manifest itself in inactivity or paralysis, but in deferring and not finishing. Behind it is a cycle, the start of which probably goes back beyond this present educational experience. However, lack of confidence and fear of failure combine with procrastination and false starts in a circling process, the one confirming the other. So despite Sarah's application and her efforts, her writing remains being endlessly drafted. In not finishing she confirms her fear that she will not finish, which can then grow in certainty and continue to undermine her.

Listening closely to the words that Sarah used during the interview opened up another insight. The word "missing" kept coming back again and again. Interestingly, such is its power that as I am writing up Sarah's case study, I too am aware of a concern that I am "missing" something. During the interview, it led to a reflection about how the physical space she works in echoes an internal chaos and about her own difficulties with addressing either. She could sort out her environment. She could use the writing journal which, in the past, she has found helps her to anchor her thoughts more securely. Yet she sidesteps both. Rereading the transcript, I begin to wonder whether her oft-repeated fear of failure is really hiding behind it a fear of success. Success could be equally unsettling. Perhaps it would mean a shift in how she or others see her. Perhaps it would mean her growing into being a "proper" academic. Perhaps it would mean her words and opinions being out there for scrutiny. Perhaps it would mean having an impact.

What this suggests is that the words we use to describe our writing blocks are significant to understanding them. Words that are repeated are of particular interest. The antonyms of the words we choose may also be useful. By exploring the meanings of the language we employ there's the potential for breaking through the superficial and into the less simplistic layers which might hold some of the answers as to why we are being held back in our writing.

Sarah's narrative unearths the emotional side of writing blocks[12]. It also displays a writing block which this time comes in the guise of activity, including, paradoxically, writing. We can be blocked in our writing and still writing, indeed enjoying writing. Sarah has little problem generating ideas, writing outlines and plans. It is the next step, when the audience comes into the picture, which closes her down. Then the idea of it having to be perfect, it having to be complete, takes over.

Our conception of the audience will be built from a reality, as well as from our imagination and from our past experiences. It is worth working out what we actually know about an audience, rather than what we think we know about it. In academia — in the marking of essays and PhDs; in the peer review of articles; in the reviewing of books — there is an element of evaluation and an onus on the author to be able to justify their position. This should be stringent. It can be harsh. On the other hand, it can also be supportive and encouraging; it can help illuminate parts of our study. The reality is mixed, allowing for a range of responses to our writing. Our imagined reality often is not. Sarah feels well supervised in her PhD; however, it has taken her some time to eschew the sense that it's "got to be perfect on the first draft, rather than just a draft". She is having to adjust her beliefs about what will be acceptable to her audience. One of the problems is that adjusting our beliefs or learning what would be welcomed by a particular audience most often happens only once we are able to put something in front of them. So again we are in a self-perpetuating pattern, this time of untested expectations getting in the way of testing the expectations.

There's a sense of having to find a place to start, as Sarah's portrayal of her writing blocks leads me to several self-feeding spirals. How to break into them? How to find something small which will just shift the balance minutely so that another pattern can be formed? Or maybe spirals are also workable. After all, spirals do not bring us back to the same exact point and can still move us forward.

I have suggested in Chapter 1 that the creative process, how we write, can be conceptualised as a spiral. It is a bumpy, uneven spiral with pauses and moments of hesitation. Maybe Sarah's present sense of blocking is akin to these. After the herculean exertions of her first chapter, she is in a lull, a hiatus. Or her lack of confidence and her anxiety about the audience are the jolts in her path which, once she knows they are there, become less noticeable or intrusive. What comes through Sarah's descriptions is a writing block which is looping, and quite dynamic in some ways. A greater understanding of the way it flows could be a key to moving through it rather than being blocked by it.

Summary box

There can be a lot of activity in a writing block.
Writing blocks may have an emotional basis.
Halts in writing may be part of a natural writing rhythm.

CASE STUDY 4: YOU'RE RESIGNING YOURSELF TO MEDIOCRITY

George[13] has just completed his first year on a general science degree. He does not like tasks which require extended writing. Though he did not explicitly reveal it, from what he said it became obvious that his attitude to writing stems at least partly from issues with dyslexia. George is an articulate, smart young man; what the interview revealed were the tender points, the vulnerabilities, he felt around writing. I have chosen to represent what he told me through three themes:

– Resigning yourself to mediocrity.
– This gift you never had.
– Wipe it all clean and start again.

Themes

Resigning yourself to mediocrity   During his final years at school George avoided subjects which required any extended writing. He was nonplussed, therefore, to discover that his degree required him to produce essays. He describes what it's like for him, beginning with his previous experience of writing essays:

> You spend ages on it and at the end of the day you finally produce a piece of work and it comes back covered in red pen. And I think that's why at "A" Level I thought, I never want to be assessed on these subjects again. And it's interesting at university when, even in a science degree, you have to do that kind of extended writing and you have to readjust and really get back into the original stuff that you thought you were rubbish at.

George describes some of the extended writing expected of him at university:

> We did book reviews on popular science writing; which was pretty good, I really enjoyed the books but I don't know, it just didn't flow for me. I mean, obviously it's not a massive issue for me because those two won't count, but I don't know, it feels a bit weird that you're going into a module with the expectation that you're probably not going to do as well as you'd hoped to. You may try, but it's quite difficult to find the motivation. As hard as you try for this, it'll probably never be as good as you anticipate or want it to be; you're kind-of resigning yourself to mediocrity from the start.

George is good at dampening down the significance of this. It is "weird", "semi-ironic", it "doesn't matter because the module marks won't count". However, as I was listening to him, feelings of frustration, even anger, came up for me. I offered him the word "frustration" and he accepted it. He recognised the psychological barrier which was there and the power of it, as well as how unhelpful it is in the academic environment.

> But if you can't get into it and you don't enjoy it and you feel that however hard you try you can't get past below average, you can't excel at it like you really want to, it's psychologically a bit defeating. ... I work so I don't do badly. I work because I need to pass this, not, you know, because I'm confident enough in this subject that I can probably do much better. I don't feel that I can probably get top marks based on the amount of work I put in. ... If

you feel enthusiastic about the subject, you feel quite passionate about the subject and then you read a piece of writing that you've written which just blatantly does not convey that in the slightest, it just feels like you've knocked something out which you've not put any effort into and it's not enjoyable to read; it feels like you're not going to get anywhere. The motivation is just not there. ... It's completely self-defeating and it's a bad trait to have in an academic environment.

The gift you never had From early on in his schooling, George was receiving negative messages about his capacity to write. If there was assistance or guidance to be had, he did not take it. He began to feel that good writing is something people are gifted with, it's something that comes naturally to some but not to others.

> Every teacher's report: Needs to work on presentation, needs to work on writing. The fundamental way of getting it onto the paper so the teacher can read what's inside your head: I think there's kind-of like a barrier there, it feels like there is. Some people just have this gift that you never had and never will have, probably. I just felt frustrated all the time: you're constantly being told that however much effort you put in it's not going to be brilliant; then, you know, you're striving for average, basically; you're striving for just above average. ... I just got into this mindset that it's just English, it's just something I'm not very good at, I'm not very good at writing generally. I probably just sort-of run myself into a bit of a wall, into a bit of a pen.

Always someone to strive for high marks, he also felt cheated. His academic progression was being blighted and not because he didn't know or comprehend the subjects he was taking, but because he didn't have the "gift" which would enable him to express his understanding.

> I used to feel it didn't test what the subject was about, like you were assigned marks for something that wasn't relevant to the subject. If you feel like you can't write particularly well or in a naturally flowing way, that's going to hinder your marks. I don't think that's fair. Yeah, that is a little frustrating.

The frustration, the sense of unfairness, fuelled George's aversion to writing. I got the impression that it — the writing or the act of writing — became something which had malicious intent. Its intent was to trip him up, to do him down. It certainly became something to be avoided.

Wipe it clean George has found strategies to help him achieve in the academic environment which have not been so reliant on writing. He has chosen subjects which required less extended writing. He takes few notes in lectures, but has become a skilled listener and uses books for revision.

> I think that's benefitted me, to realise writing's not my strong point and try and find a way of learning which is more beneficial for me.

There are downsides to these strategies, which George himself identifies. His avoidance of writing means that when he is given an extended writing task he feels ill-prepared and out of practice.

> But then when you have to do these writing tasks it doesn't set you up to do that because you're essentially working without any kind of preparation. ... If you're doing an essay-based subject and you're not used to writing down notes, not used to kind-of copying down ideas which you think are relevant, it possibly puts you at a disadvantage as compared to other people. It's a question of practice.

Word processing has been an absolute boon for George, especially being allowed to use a computer in exam situations.

> I find word processing a heck of a lot easier than physical writing and I was allowed to do that for some of my exams and because of that I produced some competent pieces of work and I was proud of them.

On the other hand, this dispensation in itself created ambivalent feelings: "because obviously you're doing it differently from other people, you think, in a way, you're cheating even though you've been granted this and this is apparently fair. ... You still feel like you're kind of cheating almost, you're getting advantage over other students."

One benefit of word processing is that "it doesn't matter if you mess up, you can wipe it all clean and start again."

> With paper you have to cross it out, you have this big horrible mark or you have to scrunch up this piece of paper and leave it on the side and I feel that you're kind-of reminded of the fact that that's not very good. Then you start panicking about how you're going to keep producing stuff. But with the computer you just wipe it clean, wipe it clean, start again completely and it's almost, you know, out of your mind. ... [With writing by hand] you keep on trying but I find a lot of the frustration builds up. It's a lot of effort and if you're constantly getting it wrong, which I tend to do, you get more flappy, a lot more flustered. I really dislike physically writing it down on paper. I find word processing a lot easier.

When I suggested that first drafts are always messy and imperfect, George responded: "I feel very, very critical of myself and so I wipe it off and write it down until I get it acceptable. I'm not a natural writer, and, you know, if it's not showing me to be good, I hate it, I really dislike it."

George did briefly touch on how starting at university could also "wipe it clean". How it was an opportunity to put previous experiences and feelings towards writing behind him; though he had, in fact, brought them with him: "and it doesn't make any sense really because everything's new, you know, everyone's new, no-one really cares what you've done in the past."

CHAPTER 7

George has struggled with writing through his education and continues to feel that his capacity to write is inadequate. He feels he does not have the "gift" and will always be working hard to reach "mediocrity". He has his own strategies for learning and for doing the tasks which are assigned to him. However, his main strategy remains avoidance. Next year he will choose "the modules which minimise [writing] as much as possible because I know I'm never particularly successful at it and I think at this point I'm not too bothered. I tried it and it didn't really work out, it's something that I'm not particularly good at, so I think the simple thing is that I'm not particularly bothered any more."

Discussion

As with the other case studies, the psychological and emotional elements come through compellingly in George's story, as does the importance of previous experiences. What impacted me powerfully was how this has led to a rejection of writing. This is a strand I will pick up here, along with a consideration of writing as a learned skill.

The rejection of writing   While I was with George, listening to his narrative, the image which came strongest to mind was one of a portcullis coming down as soon as writing came into view. At that point the writing was harmless, a gambling, playful creature, somewhere in the distance. During the transcribing and then the rereading and working with the transcription, the writing itself took on a sense of malice. It was a wily brute rather than a ferocious one, though its intent was malevolent. Its purpose was to cause George upset, to trip him up, make his life a misery. No wonder George avoids it, defensively dismissing it with phrases such as, "I'm not particularly bothered any more."

It's hard for a writer like me to hear this. It's like when someone tells you your favourite granny actually starved them of love and nourishment. Can this be true? And yet the reality of it comes through very clearly in George's language.

There is a mighty stand-off now between George and writing. And George does not appear to have any good experiences of writing to counteract the present situation, to go back to and start engaging with. This block feels as heavy and final as a portcullis.

On the other hand, George does enjoy reading, he is articulate orally and words in themselves are not unwelcome. It is the committing them to paper for himself which causes the portcullis to fall. Yet an enjoyment of words is already a foundation to work from. It is, perhaps, a place to rediscover — or discover for the first time — the "joy of writing" (see Chapter 6).

There is another rejection here, a rejection of writing as a means of assessment. "If you feel like you can't write particularly well or in a naturally flowing way, that's going to hinder your marks. I don't think that's fair. Yeah, that is a little frustrating." It came as a shock to George that writing is the basis of assessment even for what is basically a scientific degree. In academia everyone has to write. In most subjects writing is the tool rather than the thing to be studied; however, not being able to write fluently and with ease will undermine the edifice on which the studying is done. It is almost certainly possible to get through a degree without having to reveal your lack of skills with statistics. But is that possible in terms of writing? In today's academia, I very much doubt it.

Schools, colleges and universities are all putting in place supports for students who have issues around writing. George himself is benefitting, being allowed to use a word processor for some of his exams, "And because of that I produced some competent pieces of work and I was proud of them." On the other hand, there is still a question remaining: is the emphasis on assessment by the written word appropriate for all subjects? Are there, perhaps, other ways to test understanding and competency which do not need writing and which students should be encouraged to avail themselves of? Leave the portcullis where it is and find another way across the drawbridge?

Writing skills   For George, being able to write is a "gift" given to some and not to him. I feel sad even typing that, as I consider writing to be a gift for all. What seems to have passed George by almost completely is the idea that writing is a process (see Chapter 1). It is an iterative activity: we go back round what we are writing numerous times; and it requires skills which can be learnt — and, indeed, we do all learn them, develop them, continually.

George cannot tolerate the messiness of first drafts. It seems to me that his intolerance goes back to his negative early experiences of writing. He sees messiness not as a part of being creative, but as something to get red lines through and bad marks for. Crossings-out remind him of being castigated for "getting it wrong". So to tolerate the way first drafts are, and should be, would probably mean facing some of these difficult memories.

Writing, and learning to write fluently and evocatively, requires application. It also requires an apprenticeship (see Chapter 1). With luck, most of us go through this at school and are used to its exigencies as we continue our apprenticeship when we get into higher and further education. However, if we don't, then it can be hard to stop, take stock and find the time to embark on our own apprenticeship. By then we may well have come to the conclusion that we just haven't got whatever it takes. We may not be aware that it is a case of a greater understanding of our writing process (see Chapter 1) and that the skills we already have can be honed and worked on to help us become more comfortable with our writing (ideas throughout this book, but particularly Chapters 4, 5 & 6).

Summary box

Writing blocks can lead to a total rejection of writing as an activity.
Writing is a skill which can be learnt.

CHAPTER 7

CONCLUSION

I hope these case studies have given a sense of the breadth and depth of writing blocks. Each person's experience is personal to them; however, there are crossovers, especially in terms of:

- The effects of previous writing experiences.
- The responses of audiences (real, imagined, past and present).
- The importance of the emotional aspects to what is stopping them writing.

My co-researchers have found their own strategies for dealing with their writing blocks and others can be extrapolated from their experiences. These can be summarised as follows:

- Become more understanding of your writing process (see Chapter 1).
- Use a writing journal (see "Writing Strategies" Chapter 1).
- Listen to your writing blocks: they have something to tell you (see Chapters 2 & 3).
- Use new technology. As well as word processing, there are packages which can help with the organisation of information and mind-mapping (see "Writing Strategies" in Chapters 3 & 5).
- Get support. Discuss the possibility of seeking assessment by means other than writing (see Chapter 5).
- Explore creative techniques (see Chapter 6).

NOTES

[1] "Co-researcher" is a term I choose to use for my interviewee to acknowledge the co-creation of the "data" (Finlay & Evans, 2009, p. 21).
[2] Interviewees were given the choice of whether to use their real name or a pseudonym, a full name or only their first name.
[3] See Chapter 5.
[4] See Chapter 3.
[5] See Chapter 5.
[6] See Chapter 2.
[7] Interviewees were given the choice of whether to use their real name or a pseudonym, a full name or only their first name.
[8] See Chapter 2.
[9] See "parallel process" in Chapter 3.
[10] See Chapter 2.
[11] Interviewees were given the choice of whether to use their real name or a pseudonym, a full name or only their first name.
[12] See Chapter 2.
[13] Interviewees were given the choice of whether to use their real name or a pseudonym, a full name or only their first name.

CONCLUSION

A PLACE TO REST

You've reached a resting place in your journey.
There are certainly deadlines you've to meet,
yet here you may replenish your story,
take your well-earned ease, for a while at least.
Stay amongst emerald pines skirted in snow,
the chill night air flutes between the branches,
the lake shimmers, a mirror for the moon,
the owl's wingbeats are breaths in the stillness.
A thoughtful place to stop, to take your stock
of the road that together we travelled,
of the pathways you've yet to choose to take,
of loops, escarpments, sudden dips, hollows.
Knowing these moments of such precious grace
loose words, as clouds loose those crystalline flakes.

APPENDIX

THE GESTALT CYCLE

"Gestalt" is a German word which encapsulates the meaning of something being whole and completed, where the whole is greater than the sum of its parts; for example, a symphony has greater weight and resonance than it being just a collection of musical notes. The word Gestalt was appropriated by Frederick (Fritz) and Laura Perls in the 1940s to encompass a phenomenological-existential, humanistic psychotherapy that they were developing. Since the 1940s Gestalt Psychotherapy has grown to "professional, theoretical and ethical maturity". (Clarkson, 1989, p. 2.)

The aspect of Gestalt psychotherapy theory that I want to focus on here is the "Gestalt Cycle" because it is one of the inspirations for the "Creative Process" I introduce in Chapter 1.

The Gestalt Cycle suggests that every human need is met through a recurring, circular procedure constituted of the following phases which I very briefly summarise here:

- One — a resting phase, the "fertile void" from which a need emerges into the foreground. This leads to...
- Two — sensation, when our physical senses are activated.
- Three — we become aware of what we are feeling through our bodily sensations.

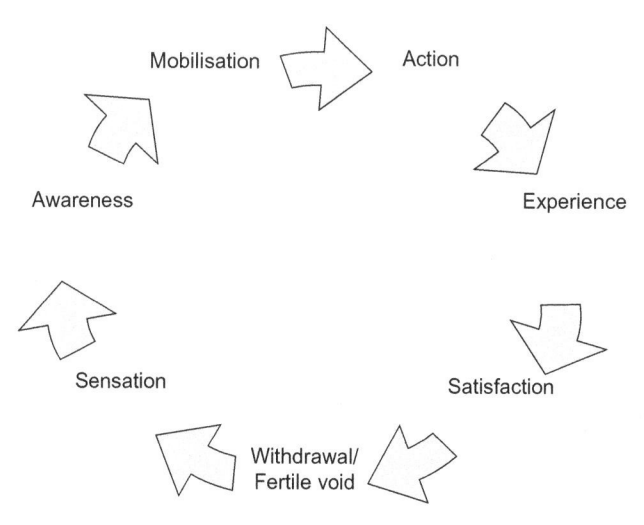

A diagrammatic representation of the Gestalt Cycle drawn from Clarkson, (1989).

APPENDIX

- Four — we mobilise and…
- Five — take action.
- Six — we fully experience our need being met.
- Seven — we feel satisfaction.
- Eight — we withdraw into the "fertile void" once more.

One of the aims of Gestalt psychotherapy would be to explore what interrupts this cycle. Interruptions to the cycle, perhaps caused by beliefs that we have inherited from others (for example, we are never good enough, so we do not feel satisfied with anything we do), mean that we do not complete our "Gestalt", we do not attain a sense of wholeness.

The main aspects I have taken from the Gestalt Cycle are "satisfaction" and the "fertile void". However, there are other crossovers: "action" and "experience" with the "aha moments" and "engagement" phases, for instance, or "sensation" and "awareness" with "idea" and "amassing".

REFERENCES

Abbott, A. (2007). Against Narrative: a preface to lyrical sociology. *Sociological Theory, 25*(1), 67–99.
Adame, A. L., Leitner, L.M., & Knudson, R.M. (2011). A Poetic Epiphany: exploration of aesthetic forms of representation. *Qualitative Research in Psychology, 8*, 370–379.
Alasuutari, P. (1995). *Qualitative Method and Cultural Studies.* London: Sage.
Alvarez, A. (2005). *The Writer's Voice.* London: Bloomsbury.
Angwin, R. (2003). Creative Spark. *Mslexia,* 18.
Antoniou, M., & Moriarty, J. (2008). What Can Academic Writers Learn from Creative Writers? Developing guidance and support for lecturers in higher education. *Teaching in Higher Education, 13*(2), April, 157–167.
Atwood, M. (2003). *Negotiating with the Dead.* London: Virago.
Barber, P. (2002). Gestalt — a prime medium for holistic research and whole person education. *British Gestalt Journal, 11*(2), 78–90.
Barks, C. with Moyne, J., Arberry, A.J. & Nicholson, R. (1995). *The Essential Rumi.* Quality Paperback Book Club.
Beard, F. (2003). The Poem that was Really a List. *Poetry in Performance, 2*(57) Productions, www.poetryjukebox.com.
Boden, M. (2004). *The Creative Mind: Myths and Mechanisms.* (2nd ed.) London & New York: Routledge.
Boice, J. & Jones, F. (1984). Why Academicians Don't Write. *Journal of Higher Education, 55*(5), 567–582.
Bold, C. (2012). *Using Narrative in Research.* Thousand Oaks: Sage.
Bolton, G. (1999). *The Therapeutic Potential of Creative Writing: Writing Myself.* London: Jessica Kingsley Publishers.
Bolton, G., Howlett, S., Lago, C. & Wright J.K. (2004). *Writing Cures. An introductory handbook of writing in counselling and therapy.* Hove & New York: Brunner-Routledge.
Bolton, G., Field, V. & Thompson, K. (Eds.) (2006). *Writing Works. A resource handbook for therapeutic writing workshops and activities.* London & Philadelphia: Jessica Kingsley Publishers.
Bowlby, J. (1988). *A Secure Base: Parent-child attachment and healthy human development.* New York: Basic Books.
Brewer, R.C. (2007). *Your PhD Thesis.* Abergele: Studymates.
Cameron, J. (1993). *The Artist's Way. A spiritual path to higher creativity.* Pan Books.
Carr, N. (2011). The Dreams of Readers. In *Stop What You're Doing and Read This!* London: Random House UK.
Cashdan, S. (1988). *Object Relations Therapy: Using the relationship.* London & New York: W.W. Norton & Company.
Clarkson, P. (1989). *Gestalt Counselling in Action.* London, Newbury Park, New Delhi: Sage Publications.
Clarkson, P (2003). *The Therapeutic Relationship* (2nd ed.) London & Philadelphia: Whurr Publishers.
Claxton, G. (2012). www.guyclaxton.com. (Accessed 26th June 2012).
Coulehan, J. (2003). Metaphor and Medicine: Narrative in clinical practice. *Yale Journal of Biology and Medicine, 76*(2), 87–95.
Csikszentmihalyi, M. (1996). *Creativity, Flow and the Psychology of Discovery and Invention.* HarperPerennial.
Csikszentmihalyi, M. (2012). www.ted.com/talks/Mihay_Csikszentmihalyi_on_flow. (Accessed 26th June 2012.)
Dark, K. (2009). Examining Praise from the Audience: What does it mean to be a "successful" poet-researcher? In Prendergast, M., Leggo, C. & Sameshima, P. (Eds.) (2009). *Poetic Inquiry. Vibrant voices in the social Sciences.* Rotterdam, Boston, Taipei: Sense Publishers.
Darnton, J. (2001). Introduction in *Writers [on Writing]. Collected essays from the* New York Times. New York: Times Books, Henry Holt & Company.
Davies, R. (1997). Parallel Processes in Organisational Consulting. *British Gestalt Journal, 6*(2), 114–117.

REFERENCES

Denzin, N.K. & Lincoln, Y.S. (Eds.) (2000). *Handbook of Qualitative Research* (2nd ed.) Thousand Oaks, London, New Delhi: Sage Publications.
DeYoung, P. (2003). *Relational Psychotherapy: A primer.* New York: Brunner-Routledge.
Dobyns, S. (2003). *Best Words, Best Order: Essays on poetry.* (2nd ed.) Basingstoke: Palgrave Macmillan.
Dunleavy, P. (2003). *Authoring a PhD: how to plan, draft, write and finish a doctoral thesis or dissertation.* Basingstoke: Palgrave Macmillan.
Eliot, T.S. (1954). Ash-Wednesday. In *Selected Poems.* London, Boston: Faber & Faber.
Evans, K. (2011). The Chrysalis and the Butterfly: A phenomenological study of one person's writing journey. *Journal of Applied Arts & Health 2*(2), 173–186.
Evans, K. (2011A). Writer's Block: a reflective literature review. *European Journal for Qualitative Research in Psychotherapy*, 5, 3–11. http://www.eurocps.eu/sites/default/files/Journal2011_i5.pdf
Evans, K. (2009). Rhythm 'n' Blues: Bringing poetry into groupwork. *Groupwork 19*(3), 27–38.
Faulkner, S. (2009). *Poetry as Method: Reporting research through verse. (Developing qualitative inquiry).* Left Coast Press Inc.
Finlay, L. (2011). *Phenomenology for Therapists: Researching the lived world.* Chichester, West Sussex: Wiley-Blackwell Ltd.
Finlay, L. & Evans, K. (2009). *Relational-centred Research for Psychotherapists: Exploring meanings and experience.* Chichester, West Sussex: Wiley-Blackwell Ltd.
Finlay, L. & Molano-Fisher, P. (2008). "Transforming" self and world: A phenomenological study of a changing lifeworld following cochlear implant. *Medicine, Healthcare and Philosophy, 11*, 255–267.
Foucault, M. (1974). *The Eye of Power.* http://foucault.info/documents/foucault.eyeOfPower.en.html (Accessed 20th February 2012).
Frank, A. (1995). *Body, Illness & Ethics.* University of Chicago Press.
Frank, A. (1997). *The Diary of a Young Girl.* (Eds. Otto H Frank and Mirjan Pressler. Trans. Susan Massotty). Penguin Books.
Furman, R. (2006). Poetic Forms and Structures in Qualitative Health Research. *Qualitative Health Research 16*(4), 560–566.
Galvin, K. & Todres, L. (2009). Poetic Inquiry and Phenomenolgical Research: The practice of 'embodied interpretation'. In Prendergast, M., Leggo, C. & Sameshima, P. (Eds.) (2009). *Poetic Inquiry. Vibrant voices in the social Sciences.* Rotterdam, Boston, Taipei: Sense Publishers.
Garner, A. (1997). *The Voice That Thunders.* Harvill Press.
Gergen, K. Ken Gergen talks about social constructionist ideas, theory and practice (http://vimeo.com/15676699). (Accessed 29th May 2012.)
Gerhardt, S. (2004). *Why Love Matters: how affection shapes a baby's brain.* Routledge.
Gilbert, M. & Evans, K. (2000). *Psychotherapy Supervision.* Buckingham: Open University Press.
Glesne, C. (1997). That Rare Feeling: Re-presenting research through poetic transcription. *Qualitative Inquiry, 3*(2), 202–221.
Godwin, G. (2001). A Novelist Breaches the Border to Nonfiction. *Writers [on Writing]. Collected essays from the* New York Times. New York: Times Books, Henry Holt & Company.
Goldberg, N. (1986). *Writing Down the Bones. Freeing the writer within.* Boston & London: Shambhala.
Hall, R.A. (1977). A Schema of the Gestalt Concept of the Organismic Flow and its Disturbance. In E. W. Smith (ed) *The Growing Edge of Gestalt Therapy.* Secaucus NJ: Citadel Press.
Hamp-Lyons, L. & Heasley, B. (2006). *Study Writing: A course in writing skills for academic purposes.* Cambridge: Cambridge University Press.
Heaney, S. (1984). *Preoccupations.* London: Faber.
Hiles, D. (2002). Narrative and Heuristic Approaches to Transpersonal Research and Practice. Paper presented to CCPE, London, October 2002. http://psy.dmu.ac.uk/drhiles/N&Hpaper.htm (Accessed 26th January 2013.)
Holloway, I. (2005). Qualitative Writing. In Holloway, I. (Ed.) *Qualitative Research.* Open University Press.
Holmes, J. (2008). Finding the Story: Narrative in psychotherapy. *The Psychotherapist, 38*, 3–5.
Hunt, C. (2007). Creative Writing for Personal Development and the "Serious Practice of Poetry". *Lapidus Quarterly,* Spring/Summer, 3–6.

REFERENCES

Huston, P. (1998). Resolving Writer's Block, *Canadian Family Physician, 44*, January, 92–97.
Ivanič, R. (1998). *Writing and Identity: The discourse construction of identity in academic writing.* Amsterdam, Philadelphia: John Benjamin's Publishing Company.
Jaynes, J. (1990). *The Origin of Consciousness in the Breakdown of the Bicameral Mind.* Penguin Books.
Johnstone, A. (1983). The Writer's Hell: Approaches to writer's block. *Journal of Teaching Writing, 2*(2), Fall, 155–165.
Jones, A. (2010). Not Some Shrink-Wrapped Beautiful Package: Using poetry to explore academic life. *Teaching in Higher Education 15*(5), 591–606.
Jones, A.C. (1975). Grandiosity Blocks Writing Projects. *Transactional Analysis Journal, 5*(4), October, 415.
Jordan, R.R. (1999). *Academic Writing Course: Study skills in English.* Harlow: Longman.
Kaufman, G. (1992). *Shame, the power of caring.* (3rd ed.) Rochester, Vermont: Schenkman Books.
Kronsky, B.J. (1979). Freeing the Creative Process: the relevance of Gestalt. *Art Psychotherapy, 6*(4), 233–240.
Laird, N. (2009). Author, Author. *Saturday Guardian Review*, 4th July.
Landy, R.J. (1996). *Essays in Drama Therapy: The double life.* London, Bristol & Pennsylvania: Jessica Kingsley Publishers.
Le Guin, U.K. (2004). *The Wave in the Mind.* Boston: Shambhala.
Leggo, C. (2005). The Heart of Pedagogy: On poetic knowing and living. *Teachers and Teaching: Theory and practice, 11*(5), 439–455.
Leggo, C. (2008). Astonishing Silence: Knowing in poetry. In Knowles, J.G. & Cole, A.L. (Eds.) *Handbook of the Arts in Qualitative Research.* Thousand Oaks, CA: Sage.
Leggo, C. (2008). The Poetry of Creativity. In R. Kelly & C. Leggo (Eds.), *Creative Expression, Creative Education.* Calgary:Detselig.
Lee, A. & Boud, D. (2003). Writing Groups, Change and Academic Identity: Research development as local practice. *Studies in Higher Education, 28*(2), 187–200.
Malterud, K. (2001). The Art and Science of Clinical Knowledge: Evidence beyond measures and numbers. *The Lancet, 358*, 397–400.
Martin, K. (2000). Merely Telling Stories? Narrative and knowledge in the human sciences. *Poetics Today, 21*(2), 293–318.
Wright Mills, C. (1959). *The Sociological Imagination.* London, Oxford & New York: Oxford University Press.
Moore, S. (2003). Writers' Retreats for Academics: Exploring and increasing motivation to write. *Journal of Further and Higher Education, 27*(3), 333–342.
Morris, B. (2012). The Art and Science of Collaboration. *The Creativity Post,* 26th April 2012. www.cretivitypost.com.
Moustakas, C. (1990). *Heuristic Research, Design, Methodology and Applications.* Newbury Park, London & New Delhi: Sage.
Murray, R. (2001). Integrating Teaching and Research Through Writing Development for Students and Staff. *Active Learning in Higher Education, 2*(1), 31–45.
Newnes, C. & Jones, H. (2005). More on Writing. *Clinical Psychology, 46*, February, 10–12.
Nurse, Sir P. (2012). The Richard Dimbleby Lecture, London, 28th February 2012.
Noor, L. (2006). Shame in the Learning Context and Supervision: What we can learn about the past and its potential to impact the present. (Exploring the potential for shame amongst a group of year 9 students constructing a learning agreement). Research presentation for a Diploma in Supervision. Scarborough Psychotherapy Training Institute. Unpublished. lydia@webnoor.plus.com
Olsen, T. (1978). *Silences.* New York: Delacorte Press/Seymour Lawrence.
Palumbo, D. (2000). *Writing from the Inside Out.* New York, Chichester, Weinham, Brisbane, Singapore & Toronto: John Wiley & Sons Inc.
Phillips, E.M. & Pugh, D.S. (2005). *How to Get a PhD: A handbook for students and their supervisors.* Open University Press.
Phillips, H. (2005). Looking for Inspiration. *New Scientist,* 29th October, 40–42.
Polkinghorne, D.E. (1988). *Narrative Knowing and the Human Sciences.* State University of New York Press.

REFERENCES

Prendergast, M., Leggo, C. & Sameshima, P. (Eds.) (2009). *Poetic Inquiry: Vibrant voices in the social Sciences.* Rotterdam, Boston & Taipei: Sense Publishers.
Prendergast, M. (2004). Ekphrasis and Inquiry: Artful writing on arts-based topics in educational research. Paper presented at the Second International Conference of the Imagination in Education Research Group, Simon Fraser University, Vancouver, British Columbia, Canada. http://www.ierg.net/pub-conf2004.php. (Accessed 5th February 2012.)
Quaytman, W. (1971). Psychotherapist's Writing Block. *Journal of Contemporary Psychotherapy, 4*(1), 53–57.
Rapport, F. (2009). Poetry of Memoir. In Prendergast, M., Leggo, C. & Sameshima, P. (Eds.) *Poetic Inquiry. Vibrant voices in the social Sciences.* Rotterdam, Boston & Taipei: Sense Publishers.
Redman, P. (2001). *Good Essay Writing: A social sciences guide.* London, Thousand Oaks & New Delhi: Sage Publications.
Richardson, L. (2000). Writing: A Method of Inquiry. In Denzin, N.K. & Lincoln, Y.S. (Eds.) *Handbook of Qualitative Research.* (2nd ed.) Thousand Oaks, London & New Delhi: Sage Publications.
Robson, D. (2010). Seeing isn't believing. *New Scientist.* 28th August, 31–33.
Romanyshyn, R.D. (2007). *The Wounded Researcher: Research with soul in mind.* New Orleans, Louisiana: Spring Journal Books.
Rothenberg, A. (1990). *Creativity and Madness: New findings and old stereotypes.* Baltimore & London: John Hopkins University Press.
Rudeston, K.E. & Newton R.R. (2001). *Surviving Your Dissertation: A comprehensive guide to content and process.*(2nd ed.) Thousand Oaks, London & New Delhi: Sage Publications Inc.
Sexton, A. (1971). *Transformations.* London: Oxford University Press.
Shinebourne, P. (2011). Poetry and qualitative psychology: The intertwining of embodiment, emotion, imagination and sense-making. Presentation at the 30th International Human Science Research Conference: Intertwining body self-world. 27th-30th July 2011, Oxford.
Sillitoe, A. (2007). The Loneliness of the Long-Distance Runner. Harper Perennial Re-issue edition.
Sinner, A. Leggo, C., Irwin, R.L., Gouzouasis, P. & Grauer, K. (2006). Arts-based Educational Research Dissertations: Reviewing the practices of new scholars. *Canadian Journal of Education, 29*(4), 1223–1315.
Spencer, S. (2011). Thoughts and Feelings. *Nursing Standard,* 2611(66).
Spencer, S. (2011). Writing My Way Out of Academic Torpor. *Lapidus Quarterly,* Summer, 13–14.
Spinelli, E. (1989). *The Interpreted World: An introduction to phenomenological psychology.* Thousand Oaks, London & New Delhi: Sage Publications.
Stern, D. (1985). *The Interpersonal World of the Infant: A view from psychoanalysis and developmental psychology.* New York: Basic Books.
Stern, D. (2004). *The Present Moment in Psychotherapy and Everyday Life.* WW Norton & Co.
Swift, G. (2009). *Making an Elephant: Writing from within.* Picador.
Taylor, C. (1989). *Sources of the Self: The making of the modern identity.* Cambridge: Harvard University Press.
Thomas, D. (1988). The Force That Through the Green Fuse Drives the Flower. *Collected Poems 1934–1953.* Everyman Classics London: J.M. Dent and Sons Ltd.
Todres, L. (2007). *Embodied Enquiry. Phenomenological touchstones for research, psychotherapy and spirituality.* Palgrave MacMillan.
Torrance, M., Thomas, G.V. & Robinson, E.J. (1992). The Writing Strategies of Graduate Research Students in the Social Sciences. *Studies in Higher Education, 17*(2), 155–61.
Torrance, P. (1995). *Why Fly? Philosophy of Creativity (Creativity Research).* Psychology Press Ltd.
Trollope, J. (2003). A Year in the Gerbil's Nest. *The Guardian.* 22nd February.
Van Manen, M. (1990). *Researching Lived Experience: Human science for an action sensitive pedagogy.* New York: State University of New York Press.
Wallin, D. (2007). *Attachment in Psychotherapy.* New York & London: Guildford Press.
Ward, A. (2011). "Bringing the Message Forward": Using poetic re-presentation to solve research dilemmas. *Qualitative Inquiry, 17*(4), 355–363.
Wellington, J. (2010). More Than a Matter of Cognition: An exploration of affective writing problems of postgraduate students and their possible solutions. *Teaching in Higher Education, 12*(2), 135–150.

REFERENCES

Winnicott, D.W. (1971). *Playing and Reality.* Penguin Books.

Wolton, R. (2006). Critic Tango: A workshop on the inner critic. In Bolton, G., Field, V. & Thompson, K. (Eds.) *Writing Works. A resource handbook for therapeutic writing workshops and activities.* London & Philadelphia: Jessica Kingsley Publishers.

Woods, P. (1999). *Successful Writing for Qualitative Researchers.* London & New York: Routledge/Falmer.

Yontef, G. (1993). *Awareness, Dialogue and Process: Essays on Gestalt therapy.* Gouldsboro, ME: The Gestalt Journal Press.

INDEX

academic writing
   apprenticeship, 24–25, 89, 101–102
   audience, 22, 39, 44–46, 122
   authentic voice, 105–107, 117
   conventions, 38, 55, 58, 64, 75, 85–87
   a creative process, 10–11
   narrative, 69, 70–72
   point of view, 64–65, 85

blocks to writing, 21–24, 41–47, 48–52, 60–64, 76, 88–89, 110
   meanings of, 61–64, 125

chunking, 18, 90
conscious mind (*see also* unconscious mind), 15
creative approach, 20–21
creative process, 11–20, 130
   aha moments, 16
   amassing, 13–15
   engagement, 17
   fertile void, 17–18
   satisfaction, 17–18
   the idea, 11–13
   waiting-muse, 15–16
creativity, 19

drafts, 17, 25, 93

editing, 17, 23
encouragement (*see also* feedback), 93

feedback, 17, 18, 25, 44–46, 47–48, 60, 88

Gestalt Cycle, 11, 17–18, 139–140

metaphor, 51, 104–105, 111–113
mind maps, 64

our first reader (*see also* self-criticism), 38, 39, 60, 110

peer review, *see* feedback
plagiarism, 88–89
planning, 17, 90–91
poetry, 94–98, 124
proofreading, 18

reflexivity, 5–7, 59
rewriting, *see* editing
role of researcher, 56, 87, 115

self-criticism (*see also* our first reader), 18, 21, 22, 23, 47, 52, 60
shame, 18, 22, 42–44
subconscious mind, *see* unconscious mind

thesaurus, 111
truth, 86–87

unconscious mind, 15, 17, 18, 20, 23, 28, 38–39

writerly self, 46–47, 60, 73–75, 89
   and imposter syndrome, 34, 46–47, 128
writing
   affective domain, 41–47, 61–62, 118, 126–127, 131–132
   attachment 55–57, 60, 74
   creative techniques, 94–98, 102–105
   distance, 57–58
   embodied, 30–32, 109
   finding words, 76, 103–104, 106–107
   flow, 20, 56
   free, 19, 28–30
   the in-between, 59
   joy of, 20, 102–103
   parallel process, 60–63

playing, 27, 29, 56, 59, 102
relationality, 38–39, 119, 121, 121–122, 125
skills (*see also* academic writing, apprenticeship), 2, 84, 132, 135
thinking through, 19, 72–73, 76, 107–110, 115
transitional significance, 56

writing exercises, 4–5, 29, 31–32, 33, 48–52, 65–67, 78–81, 94–98, 112–113
writing groups, 25, 91–94
writing journal, 13, 19, 25–28, 111, 127
writing strategies, 24–34, 47–52, 64–67, 76–81, 89–98, 111–113

Lightning Source UK Ltd.
Milton Keynes UK
UKOW04f0907100716

278002UK00010B/355/P